U-turn in the fast lane

One man's
journey
back to
God

U-turn
in the fast lane

The true life story
of Don Heron

Rebecca Dye Heron

press

Dundas, ON Canada

p r e s s

Joshua Press Inc., Dundas, Ontario, Canada
www.joshuapress.com

Editorial director: Michael A.G. Haykin
Creative/production manager: Janice Van Eck

© Cover photography by Paul Weeks
© Cover & book design by Janice Van Eck

Note: Although the major events of this story are factual, certain names have been changed.

National Library of Canada Cataloguing in Publication

Heron, Rebecca Dye, 1965–
    U-turn in the fast lane : one man's journey back to God / by Rebecca Dye Heron.

ISBN 1-894400-18-6

1. Heron, Don. 2. Criminals—Rehabilitation—Quebec (Province). 3. Automobile
thieves—Quebec—Montreal—Biography. 4. Prisoners—Quebec—Montreal—Biography.
I. Title.

HV6653.H47H47 2003   364.16'2'092   C2003–900279–9

Foreword
—by Paul Henderson

My first meeting with Don Heron was in Kingston, Ontario, where he organized a breakfast for local businessmen for the purpose of organizing a "discovery group," similar to the more than sixty groups established by the Leadership Group. The Leadership Group is an organization I founded in 1984 to impact on the business community in the areas of belief, character and action. Don led the resulting discovery group in Kingston until a career move took him to Brockville, where he has repeated the process.

At a recent meeting in Brockville, over a coffee, Don mentioned that a growth had been detected on his thyroid, but he told me that such a condition was almost always benign and he expected tests to confirm this. Not long after, Don learned otherwise, and he has since had his thyroid removed and undergone radiation therapy.

Throughout the ordeal, Don has maintained his usual positive attitude, met his professional responsibilities and continued his

Paul Henderson with Don Heron

leadership of the Brockville discovery group. He is an encouragement to Monika, his wife, and Erika and Kristina, his teenage daughters, and to me, personally, a real demonstration that faith in God works.

It was only after reading this book that I was able to understand the development and strengthening of that faith, in the trial of his ordeal in the depths of Bordeaux Prison. I am reminded by Don's story, of the powerful promises of God in Psalm 139:

> *Where can I go from Your Spirit? Or where can I flee from Your presence?...If I make my bed in hell, behold, You are there....Your hand shall lead me....If I say, "Surely the darkness shall fall on me"...Indeed, the darkness shall not hide from You, but the night shines as the day...When I awake, I am still with You.*

Don ran from a Christian home and upbringing into a life of crime and the darkness of Bordeaux Prison and discovered God, still with him. This is the story of that powerful discovery.

Paul Henderson
November 2002

Preface

I first met Don Heron, who is my husband's cousin, nearly fifteen years ago. He was the guest speaker at a youth event in downtown Montreal. I was impressed with his story, and its powerful testimony to God's sovereign grace. We were living in separate cities and didn't have much contact during the next several years, so I was surprised when he called and asked me to consider writing a book based on his experiences. Then, he told me about the incident that led to his call. Just at the time he was praying God would guide him to the right person, he opened a magazine and recognized my photo with an article I had written. This prompted him to pick up the phone and make the call that, to me, seemed out of the blue. We're both convinced that, far from being a coincidence, these circumstances were providential.

The main events in the story are factual, however certain names have been changed. I took a little poetic license with some of the minor events and much of the dialogue and, of course, with the inner workings of the characters' minds. The letters are actual excerpts from those Don wrote to Monika during his prison term.

I feel as if I've taken a journey with Don and Monika through some dark and difficult days: I know it hasn't been easy for them to relive these experiences. But the darkness of those times provides a wonderful foil for the light that God has brought into their lives, when he drew them to faith in and love for the Lord Jesus.

Rebecca Dye Heron
April 2002
Antwerp, Belgium

Acknowledgements

From Rebecca...
Many people have made valuable contributions to the writing of this book. I especially want to thank my family, who cheerfully kept the home fires burning during all those hours I sat at the computer. Thanks also to Don and his family, who made the writing of this book an exciting adventure; and Dan Bengtsson, who persistently hounded me to keep things moving, always asking how he could help. And finally, I thank Margaret Buchanan and Ginette Cotnoir, my extraordinary friends, who critiqued the manuscript, offered their insights and never failed to encourage me, while they drank coffee and I drank tea.

From Don...
I am indebted to so many people for their help and encouragement over the years. Thank you, Mom and Dad, for giving me the best

upbringing a child could have. Thank you, Erika and Kristina, for your loving support. Thank you, Monika, for loving me and for believing in our future even through the toughest times. Thank you, God, for making yourself so real to me.

Courage is fear
holding on a
minute longer.
—George S.
Patton

01

The picket line

The December night was cold and windy, and Don Heron was scheduled for an all-nighter on the picket line. His hands were red and chapped; his nose felt frozen when his turn came to duck into one of the tiny heated trailers for a break. The noise was deafening in the smoke-filled cabin, and within five minutes it felt too hot—the trailer was narrow and far too small for the sixteen men who were packed in like sardines.

They were mechanics, welders, machinists and millwrights—all French-speaking blue-collar workers for Brasco Steel, the giant steel plant that dominated the small Quebec town. Twenty-two-year-old Don was a class C millwright and he worked day shift. He was hired on to assist the old man who had ascended through the ranks all the way to class A. Most of the day he followed him around, pulling the man's tool box behind him in a wagon. But three months after he started, the union called a strike, and in the dead of winter he found himself doing night shifts on the picket line, when he should have been back in his apartment in a warm bed.

Just inside the door of the trailer, six men were cursing the Canadian government. They were strong supporters of the separatist movement, which was gaining momentum in Quebec. Four men at the other end, beers in their fists, were engrossed in a game of cards. Some others were laughing loudly at recycled jokes.

Don poured himself some steaming coffee and squeezed into a seat against the right-hand wall. The guy next to him dozed off, then jerked awake in embarrassment when his head rolled over onto Don's shoulder.

At 2:00 A.M., just as he was drifting into a state of semi-consciousness himself, he heard the sound of an engine. "Nice car," someone whistled, as five of the top union executives got out. The tiny trailer shook as the men opened the door and stomped in, letting the cold wind blow in with them. The noisy room became deathly still in a moment, and the picketers watched as all five leaders squeezed their way into the seats surrounding Don. The biggest of the five, a giant of a man, sat directly across from Don and stared at him, his eyes never leaving Don's face. Don, who was just over five-feet-eight, could feel the colour drain from his face and his mouth go dry, as his eyes moved up from the knees and over the muscular frame of the man, well over six-feet tall, who sat across from him and leaned heavily into him.

"We heard some news that doesn't make us very happy," the man growled. "Found out you work for the Quebec provincial police as an undercover agent. You're reporting all our activities."

Don was stunned. He had lived this scene over and over again in his nightmares. Every dream ended the same way—his lifeless body was taken through the woods, his stiff feet fitted with concrete boots and he was dumped into the St. Lawrence River—no one ever to hear of him again. He tried to keep his eyes steady, as his mind raced—frantically searching for a way out. His mind leapt toward the door, but he forced his body to stay still; forced his eyes to look straight ahead, knowing one false move could mean the realization of his nightmare. Was there any way, any way, at all, he could reach the door and make a run for it? Then he felt the men, all five of them, lean in toward him. He knew that every eye in the place was on him. There was no chance he could get away.

This was crazy. It was more than suspicion; they must be sure, or they wouldn't risk confronting him in front of all the others. Should he confess the whole thing and plead for his life? And yet, they thought he worked for the police—they obviously didn't know the whole story. Maybe it was a bluff, after all. He knew that unless they were absolutely positive, they wouldn't touch him. To harm someone in the brotherhood and then find out he was innocent would be political suicide for them. They wouldn't take any chances.

It struck him that this was the zenith of his career—the culmination of all his training. At this moment, all he had learned would carry him or it would fail him, and then…time seemed to stand still as he quickly, silently surveyed his options once again. The tension rose and hung there, suspended for a split second, and then in one giant breath he breathed it in and blew it out in a loud, wild laugh. "You caught me," he said, and the sureness and humor in his voice surprised even him. "How did you know? I'm a *spy* for the police and you're under arrest!"

The union guy across from him looked startled for a moment, and Don watched him, still laughing, hoping the shaking he felt inside wouldn't well up into his voice or leak out into his hands. Then the giant's tense face relaxed into a smile, and someone sitting at the table started laughing, too. They all laughed, and the big man slapped Don on the knee. "Just a test," he said. All five men got up and left.

This is crazy, Don thought. *Get me out of here!* But he knew he was stuck there—he had to finish the job he had started. Twelve months earlier, when he had taken this assignment, Stew Lawson had told him things would get hot, and he was right. But they could be worse—at least his corpse wasn't rotting on the bottom of the St. Lawrence River.

A slip of the
foot may soon
be recovered,
but that of
the tongue,
perhaps never.
−unknown

02
Undercover

It was a clear, sunny day just before Christmas, one year before Don's encounter in the trailer with the union leaders. He and Monika were lying on their waterbed, talking about their recent move to Montreal and wondering where his new career would take them.

From the time he was a teenager, Don knew that he wanted to be a private investigator. He studied law and security administration in college, and soon after graduation accepted a job as a claims investigator with an insurance agency in northern Ontario.

He and Monika, childhood sweethearts, got married. Two months later, when he received a job offer as an undercover investigator, he jumped at the opportunity. The newlyweds moved into an apartment in Montreal in September, and Monika began studying early childhood education at Vanier College.

His first assignment as an undercover agent was to report on the drug activity in a nearby college. He had always looked young for his age, with his compact, powerful build and his clean-cut good looks. He made a convincing "student" and hung around with the right people. He managed to get the information his employers wanted. But now he was ready for something bigger.

Don watched Monika, lying there beside him. He saw the same sweet smile and the same delicate porcelain doll-like features he had first fallen in love with as a boy. They loved their life together. Loved their late-night dinners in downtown Montreal and their not-so-early morning talks in bed. Loved their plush apartment, with its spectacular view of St. Joseph's Oratory.

They could see the dome now, over the park, through the curtainless fifth-storey window. The rays of sun streamed into the room and turned the hardwood floors into strips of gold. "This is the life. Can it get any better than this?" Don asked himself. He pulled Monika close and kissed her, savouring the warmth of her.

The phone rang.

"Donny, get down here now. Got a case—perfect for you." It was Stew Lawson, his boss. His voice sounded gruff and slurred, as usual. *He's half in the bag again, even at*—Don looked at his watch—*eight o'clock in the morning.* But he could sense Stew's excitement. "Can't tell you anything over the phone but, kid, you're going undercover."

Don was out of bed before Monika could even turn over. "This is it, Moon!" It had been his nickname for her, for as long as he could remember. "The break I've been waiting for. I can tell by Stew's voice." He pulled on his jeans and grabbed a shirt off the back of a chair. "They want me to go undercover on a big one. Didn't give me any details. Got to get to the office."

Eagle was the biggest industrial-espionage company in the world, but you'd never guess it. They purposefully kept a low profile. They had two types of investigators. Graded agents carried a gun and were given the usual short-term assignments, such as collecting evidence for defense lawyers. They often trailed a spouse, to dig up evidence for a divorce.

Don was a special agent, the second type. Although licensed to carry a gun, he kept nothing on him that could tie him to the company. It was rare for him to meet his boss in person at the office. He glanced around the outside of the building before he entered.

Stew was dark haired, short and stocky. A chain smoker and a heavy drinker, he was the stereotypical seasoned investigator. He was also a heart attack looking for a place to happen. "Glad you're here, Heron," he rasped. "Wait 'til you see what I have for you. It's Brasco, the big-time steel plant in St. Croix, Quebec, an hour and a half from Montreal. They've been having union problems—workers have formed one of the most radical unions in North America. The vice-president—name's Paul Dubé—wants an agent to hire on as a millwright and infiltrate the union." His voice was still slurred, as it had been on the phone. Don knew Stew drank to avoid his problems—his family life was a mess. Well, who could blame him?

"This is a top-secret case, Donny. Make sure you keep the details away from your family. These thugs have a bad habit of 'intimidating' parents and siblings and wives, when they smell a rat. No one in the factory except Dubé—from the guys on the line to the top brass—will know who you really are. Monika will stay here, of course. This is a round-the-clock job. Some of your 'activities' will take place at 3 or 4 A.M. Not in places she'd want to be." He winked. "You'll be one of the guys, Donny, and these guys are no angels, that's for sure."

Monika not go? Funny—he hadn't thought about that, at all. He had been waiting for something like this to come up for so long, that all the little details didn't seem to matter. Of course, Monika wouldn't want to move, anyway. She had her life—her classes, her friends, her aerobics. He could come home some weekends, and the assignment shouldn't last long.

"You'll be there three months," Stew pulled some tapes out of his briefcase and slid them onto the desk. "This is your new identity—fabricated, of course, except for your name and your family. You have three weeks to learn the stuff. Eat, sleep and drink this tape, until you can recite the facts in your sleep. You worked for eight months for Allen's Truck Lines, you studied mechanics at a two-year college and so on. You'll apply for the job as a millwright on

January 2. You'll get the job, of course, but you'll have to go through the interview, the test, fill out an application form just like the next guy. By the way, there really will be a 'next guy.' They'll hire someone else—the real thing—the same day. It'll look less suspicious if they get a kid with a similar background to yours at the same time.

"You'll have to think on your feet, Heron. Never forget what you're up against. Some of these union types would sooner kill ya than look at ya. If they discover who you are, do I need to spell it out for you? One of three things will happen. They'll bribe you with big bucks to work for them as a double and feed us false information. Or they'll expose you at a meeting—there's a spy amongst us—and make an example of you. That means they'll beat the heck out of you or kill you. Or here's the third possibility— you'll vanish into thin air and never be found. Which probably means your weighted corpse will be dropped in some stinkin' river and left to rot for fish bait on the bottom. These guys aren't playing games, so you're not, either.

"Get an apartment with two exits—you may need the second one for an escape route. You'll get a double salary—from us and from Brasco, the normal millwright's salary. We'll pay for all your expenses, no questions asked. Whatever the heck you do, don't get a receipt when you go out drinking with the guys. They'll be on to you before you can reach the door of the bar.

"It's uncanny the way they can spot a spy. They keep a list of suspicious characters—relatives and friends of management, people unsympathetic toward unions and all new employees. That's you.

"You'll contact the vice-president directly. Any union information or illegal activity you can uncover, you'll feed to him. Start with identifying the key players in the union."

Lose no time;
be always
employed in
something
useful.
–Benjamin
Franklin

03
Who am I?

In January of 1982, the political climate in Canada was as hot as the weather was cold. French-speaking Quebec was dissatisfied with the status quo. René Lévesque, premier of Quebec, had a vision of an independent French-speaking nation, and he was able to capture people's imagination in a way no other politician had done in years. The separatist movement was growing rapidly. The province was moving quickly toward a referendum, which many thought would lead to the breakup of Canada.

The country was entering a recession. Interest rates were high; inflation was up. Companies were negotiating low-salary contracts with their employees. The workers, nearly all French-speaking, were passionate about their language; passionate about their culture. The factory, big business, belonged to the English, but the union was theirs. The union was for the people.

Paul Dubé, vice-president Brasco Steel, understood the growing power of the union and it scared him. Three years earlier, during a major dispute, the union had hired professional hit men to shoot out the plant windows and intimidate management. The present leaders were regional men, brought in from Montreal to settle disputes. They were hard men, some of them with criminal backgrounds. They taught the workers chants—loud and angry and full of vulgarities. The place was a time bomb. So he hired bodyguards for himself, his wife and his children, and he hired Don to act as his eyes, ears and nose inside the factory.

Don was the right person for the job. As he sped down the highway toward his new assignment, he thought how all the events from his past had perfectly prepared him for the role he was about to play. His dad had come to the province thirty years before, when he was in his early twenties. He had married Don's mother, an English-speaking Quebecker—or anglophone—and together they had settled into a predominantly French community in northern Quebec. Don and his four sisters had been the only English-speaking kids on the street. He had picked up French quickly, and he could throw the words around as skilfully as he could hit the puck into the net during their street hockey games.

He had his first view of St. Croix in early January. It was a small town on the north bank of the St. Lawrence River. When he crossed the bridge and drove down the main street, he could see Brasco Steel on the left. It was a sprawling two-storey building, professionally landscaped in the front, with tinted glass windows, newly replaced after the shootings of the previous union dispute. The roar of truck motors was constant as drivers pulled up, loaded the trailers with steel products and drove away.

Don carefully filled out an application, repeating to himself the false information. He was so brainwashed, he almost believed the stuff himself. Allen's Truck Lines, he printed in the space provided for work experience. He knew Eagle Security was absolutely thorough. They had to be—the union had the right to question any application and call the reference numbers given. Allen's Truck Lines was a front company, created by Eagle for this purpose. If someone dialed the number, the name of the front company would

Don's Quebec Private Investigator's Licence

light up on Eagle's switchboard and the secretary would answer, "Allen's Truck Lines," at the other end. The thought made him smile. He almost hoped someone would try.

Then he went through a physical examination, took a test and had an interview. Later that day, he was told to report to work in one week to start his new job.

He arrived a week later at 7:00 A.M., and was put to work immediately as an assistant to a limping old man who fixed broken machinery. "Stay with me, kid," the man grunted. So Don followed him into a massive room with high ceilings and noisy machinery. It was the place where they melted down the steel, and the heat from the process was stifling. Don followed the man around with his tool box, handing him a wrench or a screwdriver when he needed it. As they went from one area to the next, he thought the plant would never end. *Not a bad idea*, he thought, as he saw a foreman whiz past him on a bike to get to the next huge section.

Don could spot the strong union men immediately, and he managed to strike up a conversation with a few of them while the old man grunted under some machinery. They were talking, when a tall heavy-set man in a suit strode into the room, looking around. "There's the enemy, Heron," the union guy whispered. "One of the top brass—Dubé. Just look at the stuck-up pig."

Don looked at Dubé curiously, a half smile on his face at the irony of the situation. He had spoken with Dubé several times on the phone. He felt that he knew him well, but he had never seen him in person. The VP had probably come onto the floor to check him out. *If these guys only knew why I'm really here*, he thought, *and who really is the enemy.* It was an odd sort of game, but he loved it. It kept him on the edge of the cliff, with his heart racing and his adrenaline pumping—a place he had always loved to be. Now he knew what his real job was and he was eager to get going—to get to know these guys and work his way into the inner circles of the union.

During coffee break in a noisy combination workshop/machine shop, he met Daniel, the cover-up who was the real millwright, hired at the same time as Don. *Nice guy*, he thought. They talked about their new jobs and their families. Don was free to discuss his real family—it was too dangerous for an agent to fabricate a family.

"Heron?" Daniel said. "Where did you say you're from? You don't happen to be related to Murray Heron, the preacher from around there, do you? The one who did time in prison for…"

Don interrupted him quickly, admitting that Murray Heron was his father. He groaned inwardly. His father's reputation had followed him all his life. Even here, even now that he was working undercover, he couldn't get away from it. He couldn't lie, though— it would be too great a risk. He changed the subject.

But Daniel wouldn't drop it. He kept pumping him with questions about his dad. Then he asked, "So, what do you think about God?"

"God who?" Don almost said, and thought it would be funny. But he took one look at Daniel's face and changed his mind. This guy was serious, he could tell. He lit a cigarette as he listened to Daniel recount the stories he had heard about his dad, all of them true. Then he told Don about how he had become a Christian.

Don knew the language, of course. He had heard it all his life. But for Daniel it was new and exciting. *Blah, blah, blah. Yeah, yeah, yeah. This is the last thing I need. I've got to get rid of this guy*, Don thought. He blew smoke in Daniel's face. Daniel ignored the smoke and told him excitedly about how much better his life was now.

Don cursed inwardly as he put out his cigarette and stood up, picking up his tool box. God, again! No matter where he went, he was there! It was as if God was haunting him or hounding him. Now this guy, this man so enthusiastic about playing church, would probably feel compelled to share his testimony with him at every coffee break and through every lunch hour. It was like some cruel practical joke.

What did this remind him of? Some memory from somewhere, way in the back of his mind, was tugging at him. Before he could stop them, irritating Bible verses from somewhere in his past flooded his mind. They were written by somebody who must have had that same haunted feeling, written directly to God. *Where can I flee from your presence? If I go up to the heavens, you are there; if I make my bed in the depths, you are there....If I say, "Surely the darkness will hide me and the light become night around me," even the darkness will not be dark to you; the night will shine like the day, for darkness is as light to you....* "Shut up!" he said out loud. And that was the last time, for a long time, he thought about the Scriptures.

Once Don figured out who the most active union members were, Dubé had him placed on work sites with them. It was after he put in his hours as a millwright that his favourite part of the job began. The guys hung out together, often partying at strip joints. He had learned, in his training, how to drink without getting drunk. There were things you could do, such as taking a teaspoon of vegetable oil to coat your stomach or sneaking a glass of water between drinks. This way, he could drink heavily with the guys and stay somewhat sober—and extract the information he wanted from them.

Whatever information he got, he passed along to Dubé, who had what they called a red phone—a special line that Don could use to reach him any time, day or night. This was a decade before cellphones were even heard of. They spoke every day, sometimes several times a day. He also wrote daily reports and sent them to a post-office box in Montreal, an address that was difficult to trace to Eagle Security. Each day, someone would pick up the report from the post office, edit it and forward a copy to Dubé at home. In the meantime, Don became known as a loyal union member at Brasco Steel.

Philippe Gagnon was a machinist and active in the union. "Hey,

Heron, ya comin' over tonight?" He yelled over the roar of the equipment, one afternoon in February. Don often dropped into his place to watch a hockey game. "It must be hard to be so far away from your wife. Family's everything, man."

Philippe was a great guy, active in the union. Too bad he was on the wrong side. Or was he? *All this partying must be burning up brain cells,* Don thought. *I'm not sure which side is right any more.* That weekend, Philippe and his wife went with Don and Monika to the Spaghetti Factory and a German pub in Montreal. They had a great time.

As his friendship with Philippe grew, so did Don's uneasiness about the role he was playing. He was beginning to feel like a real rat, betraying his friends.

One day he saw Daniel sitting alone during his break, reading a Bible. "What's the matter, can't leave home without it?" Don laughed at him.

Daniel smiled. "I'm hooked, Heron." Don grinned back at him. He couldn't help it. One part of him was annoyed with Daniel's Christian zeal, but another side was beginning to like him. Anyone who could take the things Don threw at him as calmly as Daniel did, couldn't be all bad.

One morning, a few weeks later, he got word that the workers planned a walkout for that afternoon. Union walkouts cost the company a fortune, because when the line workers left, they left all the machinery on, and it was a difficult time-consuming task for the foremen to stop production.

When Don learned about it, he immediately slipped away and called Dubé, who was able to spread the word to the foremen. They couldn't stop the walkout, but they were able to decrease production and stop the machinery early on, saving a lot of money.

Time passed quickly. Union activity was fairly quiet and Don felt good about his work. He was secure in his secret identity and he could tell the VP was pleased with the job he was doing. Most of all, he enjoyed the double salary—and all the things the money could buy.

It was at the end of his three months, when he should have gone back home to Monika, that the strike was called and the real war began.

When you're
safe at home,
you wish you
were having an
adventure;
when you're
having an
adventure, you
wish you were
safe at home.
−Thornton
Wilder

04

The union

The Quebec provincial police riot squad marched in like a silent army. Clubs in one hand, shields in the other, the squad members were like robots. There was no eye contact, as they formed long lines and inched forward in rhythm, one tiny step at a time. Then they started chanting a snarling mantra, a grunt, really, but all together and in perfect time. It was a chilling sight for the crowd of angry union workers, and very slowly, to the same rhythm as the marching squad, they backed up and gave way, leaving a narrow path, through which management was escorted into the building.

The riot squad had already been called in several times, since the morning in early spring when Don had arrived at work to find the doors of the factory locked and the strike announced. This cooling off of the heated workers was just temporary, Don knew. The union was strong and the passions of the workers were being aroused almost to a frenzy. The assemblies were more and more frequent now. Throughout that spring, summer and fall, rallies were calculated to nudge too-passive men into open hostility and to motivate them to express their feelings. The tactics were working—emotions on the picket lines and in the demonstrations were running high, and the union workers were doing all they could to fan the flames with their red-hot rhetoric.

Don was allowed in on most of the nighttime activities—he helped with the manufacturing of weapons. They altered and welded four-inch nails together, so that when thrown, they would land with the sharp ends up and flatten the tires of the managers' vehicles as they drove by. They filled baby-food jars with paint to throw at them, too. They laughed as they watched the startled men's faces, when the paint exploded on their cars or, occasionally, over their expensive suits.

During one meeting, Don learned that the organizers planned to blow up a company truck full of merchandise. The union was irritated that some production was still possible during the strike. Product going out the door meant profit. He notified Dubé, who called the police. They hid on top of the building, waiting to catch the men in the act.

But the union guys were nervous, and they knew from experience how, when and where to spot the police. They saw them on the roof in time, and they stopped the plan. The police were irritated that they couldn't make any arrests. And the activists were furious, for they knew that someone had tipped off the police.

Maybe that was when they began to suspect Don. He was well aware that his name was on the list of possible informants his boss had warned him about. And he knew the list got shorter as time went on. He figured his name was on the short list now, and he had the feeling he was being watched very carefully. It was a disturbing sensation.

A union leader approached Don. The men planned to go around and smash windows of managers' homes and wanted to use his car. When he quickly complied, Don saw a quick flash in the man's eyes and a movement in his jaw. Had he expected Don to say no?

The police were informed and caught the guys, but they didn't press charges, because they knew about Don's part in the vandalism. They were convinced that the union was testing his loyalty and that by offering his car he had passed the test.

But that was just the first test. The second one was that cold night in the trailer with the picketers, one year after Don began working for Brasco.

The event shook him up, but it was the last time Don felt pressure from the union. He hoped they had crossed his name off the short list. Maybe that hope gave him extra confidence. After that night, he began to feel invincible and he starting doing things that, had he been caught, could have gotten him into trouble on both sides of the law.

He knew one of the union executives had a briefcase full of the latest plans and strategies, and he knew where he kept it. He broke into the man's car, "borrowed" the papers, photocopied them and returned them to the car. The owner never found out. Don gave the copies to Dubé.

The vice-president was convinced that the real objective of the union was not to help the workers but to put the factory out of business. Because Brasco Steel was prospering, it was the enemy of the people.

Everything Don heard at the assemblies supported this theory. As time went on, the real agenda of the union became less and less hidden. Don decided to tape one of the meetings, using a hidden recorder. He winced as he slipped the wire under his shirt, thinking of what would happen to him if he got caught.

When he arrived at the meeting, someone handed him a large brochure announcing the International Manifestation of the Marxist-Leninist Party—on the occasion of the fourth Congress of the Communist Party of Canada. It was to be held in Montreal a few days later. He taped the entire meeting and reported what he heard.

He talked to Dubé every day and often in the middle of the night. They developed a strong alliance, but Don only met him one time in person.

It was a rendezvous that Stew Lawson set up between the three of them. They met in a motel room in a nearby town, each of them arriving at a different time, through a different door. Don came in a taxi, the last of the three to make his appearance. They talked for two hours, then left as cautiously as they had arrived.

That night, Stew and Don drank together at a local bar. Stew treated him, and in spite of Don's experience in the drinking-and-extracting-information business, Stew managed to turn the tables on him. Don got stoned and Stew pumped him for information. Although he had no real reason to doubt Don's integrity, he was still suspicious. He wanted to know for sure that Don hadn't gone over to the other side; that he wasn't a double agent. In this field, nobody trusted anybody, and Eagle Security made it their business to investigate their investigators.

Don's mind and speech were blurred and his memory of the whole incident was fuzzy, but he must have passed the test. Soon after, the dispute was settled and he was offered a three-year contract to stay on as a millwright/spy for Brasco Steel.

One may smile
and smile, and
be a villain.
—William
Shakespeare

05

The good life

Don knew that the three-year offer would probably stretch into a lifetime. In the industrial-espionage business, the longer an undercover agent stayed on one case, the more effective he was; and that was what management wanted. His front would become so convincing that he would begin to believe his own lie.

When the strike ended and the dispute was settled, there were no clear winners. The few extra cents an hour the union had coaxed from management couldn't compensate for the losses brought on by a strike that lasted more than a year. And Don felt burnt out. His three months at Brasco had expanded into fifteen months, and he was tired of the job. He felt he had completed his work there— three or four men were in prison because of criminal activity he had disclosed and several others had been fired, including his friend, Philippe Gagnon.

He should have felt satisfied about the assignment. Lawson and

Dubé had been pleased. But he couldn't shake the feeling that things weren't really as black-and-white as he had always assumed. Maybe black was white and white was black, or at least both were varying shades of gray.

Dubé had told Don how one man had been fired. Management had to step carefully, to avoid the sensitive toes of the union officials. They couldn't fire workers because they were overly zealous members of the union, so the foreman had planted something in his lunch box and accused him of theft. That was one clear reason for termination with which the union couldn't argue. But it left Don feeling uneasy.

He and Monika had rented a new apartment on the West Island of Montreal during his assignment. Now, he was ready to get back there and settle into their real lives, to stop pretending to be something he wasn't. He instinctively felt that now was the time to bail out, that if he stayed longer his cover could be blown, and then what?

Once he decided he wanted out of the contract, the difficulty was backing out gracefully—without blowing his cover and facing the possibility of being hunted down. After informing Stew and Dubé of his decision, he began planting the idea of leaving in the minds of the men at work. "Monika wants to settle down in Montreal," he would say. Or, "I'm getting a little tired of this place. I think I'll look around for another job." When the time came, his departure went unnoticed.

He was elated, the day he drove back to the city of Montreal. That night, he and Monika drove up Mount Royal in their silver Firebird, listening to music. They stopped high above the city and looked out over the rooftops. They loved the city and the world it opened up for them—the great shopping, good restaurants and exciting nightlife. That night, as they looked out over the lights of the city, they felt on top of the world.

Don leaned his head back against the headrest. "It's great to be back here, Moon."

"So what's your next case?"

"You know, I'm pretty sick of this whole undercover business.

It's risky, and each contract I take, each new identity I have to fake, will get riskier. Sooner or later, someone is bound to recognize me or catch me contradicting myself. How many backgrounds can one person have?"

Soon after that he took on a contract with the International Bureau of Investigation. His first job was from 12 to 4 A.M. at a huge nightclub in downtown Montreal. There were three levels— a gay cruising bar, a male strip bar and a discotheque that claimed the distinction of being the biggest in North America.

Don's job was to protect the money while employees counted it and escort the manager to the bank after closing at 4 A.M. He was civilian dressed, but he had a twelve-gauge pump-action shotgun in his hand and a trained attack dog at his side.

While he worked part-time on contract as an investigator, he became interested in the real estate business. He took a course and began to build a clientele. Monika had a new job as a dental assistant for two Westmount orthodontists.

One spring night, a couple of months after Don's return to Montreal, he and Monika were eating at their favourite restaurant. "Did I ever tell you about the time I sold my dog?" He asked Monika. She shook her head, smiling and curious. "Well, you know my dad's TV show?" He didn't have to tell her about that. They had grown up in the same town, and she had known his family well. She and Janice, his sister, were still best friends. Monika had even appeared on his dad's show, on several occasions when the youth group would sing.

"One night, when I was about six, my dad came home and asked if my puppy and I would like to make an appearance on the next broadcast. We both—the puppy and I—agreed enthusiastically. We got all cleaned up for the show, and we must have been impressive, because my dad received lots of mail that week—mostly about my dog. One man even offered to buy him. I considered the offer and decided I couldn't turn it down. So the man walked away with the celebrity dog, and I pocketed ten bucks."

Monika laughed. "See, even then you couldn't resist a quick profit."

"Hey, there's no sin in profit," Don shot back.

Don had lots of good childhood memories, but somehow, gradually, as he grew into his teen years, his parents' Christianity seemed too restrictive for him. There was so much he wanted to do. And something inside pushed him on to experience all he could.

Now they were far removed from all the limitations he had felt at home. For them, Christianity was a thing of the past. Don and Monika knew how to have a good time; how to enjoy life. They were young, they were both making money, and they knew how to spend it.

"Don, do you think we'll ever be able to afford to buy one of those nice houses you show with waterfront property, like the ones in Beaconsfield?" Monika asked Don, just as a waiter set down two plates of barbecued ribs. "Mmm, that smells great!"

Don grinned. "Before we furnish too many dream homes, we better make some money."

He jumped, startled, as the waiter clamped a big hand down on his shoulder. He looked up at the tall man with glasses and light brown hair, blade thin and receding in the front. The man had a contagious laugh, and Don liked him right away. "This is my kind of conversation. I always like to talk about making money. What sort of work are you in?"

Don explained his new real estate business, and the waiter was interested immediately. When the restaurant cleared out, he joined them at the table and they discussed the housing market and mortgage rates. Don was impressed with his knowledge on the subject. They shook hands, when he and Monika got up to leave. "Don't stay away too long," he called after them.

They didn't. They ate there often, over the next while. They got to know most of the waiters there and especially B.J. Cameron, the friendly waiter who, it turned out, was an ex-policeman.

> Since the house
> is on fire, let us
> warm ourselves.
> —Italian saying

06

Body bag Monday

Monika dragged herself out of bed, the Monday morning after they returned home from vacation. *Why is it that you always feel totally wiped out on your first day of work, after you've just rested up for two weeks?* She groaned when she saw the clock. *I'm already half an hour behind schedule!*

She pulled a wrinkled white uniform out of the basket of unsorted laundry, fixed her hair, then ironed the outfit. She glanced enviously at Don, who was still sleeping soundly. Then she gave him a quick kiss on the cheek, and skipping breakfast, ran out the door.

She was half asleep throughout the one-hour bus ride to the dental office where she worked. For just a moment, as she pulled the bell cord and prepared to get off at the corner of Sherbrooke and Decarie, she wondered whether or not she had unplugged the iron.

What is that smell? It smells like… Who is that standing in the doorway? Oh, it's you, Dad. Good. "Donny, I have some bad news…." The chapel burnt down? The chapel at Camp Opasatica? The chapel we built, Dad? No, no, no! It can't be, Dad. We worked too hard on it. "Son, when our work is done and it seems there's nothing else we can do—that's when things really get exciting. It's when God can take over and we can expect miracles."

But why is it still burning, even after we rebuilt it? It's so hot! Is it another fire? At the mines? Yes, I remember, now. Later, at the mine. Trapped in a long hallway…smoke from the smelter…poisonous gas…getting through my gas mask…can't breathe…must get air! Climbing out the window—third floor. Smoke pouring out…still can't breathe. Climb out onto the ledge…don't fall…hang on until the gases are gone. They're gone! But I still can't breathe.

It's so, so hot. Too hot, burning hot. "Wake up, Son. We have lots of work to do." Can't, Dad, too hot. Wake up, Son. Wake up!!"

Don woke up with a jerk. His body felt scorched, as if he had been in the sun too long. There were sirens wailing and alarms ringing in the distance, but here in the apartment he could hear the crackle of flames, devouring the furniture and the curtains. The room was incredibly bright—it was like watching colour TV come to life. But, above everything else, there was the sensation of overpowering heat.

He jumped out of bed and stepped, naked, out onto the balcony. He looked down and saw a few fire trucks and a crowd of people gathering, faces lifted toward him. He leapt back into the apartment, grabbed a housecoat and ran, through the flames, out the door. Then, he took the long way out of the building and used the elevator to get to the main floor. The moment he stepped out of the main doors, he heard an explosion and the sound of smashing glass. He looked up to see that their living room windows had just blown out, from the heat of the fire inside.

It was a strange feeling, to stand in the crowd of people and hear them excitedly speculate about the cause of the fire, whose apartment it was and if someone remained inside. He stood there for a few minutes, too stunned and too embarrassed to say anything. He watched, as if still in a dream, as a fire truck moved into position beside the pool and hoisted up a man in a box with a hydraulic arm to hose down the fire—the water came out with such force that it sprayed from the balcony of the apartment to the back wall of the living room. In a few minutes, the fire was extinguished and nothing but black foul-smelling smoke poured from the apartment.

It suddenly struck Don that he was responsible for all this commotion and he ought to confess it to someone. He found a police officer and told him the fire was in his apartment.

"Was anyone else in there with you, sir?"

"Well, no," Don answered a little sheepishly, "nobody except our little yellow budgie."

The officer held up his little finger. "Your bird's lungs are about the size of the tip of my baby finger. He died long before the flames ever touched him."

Don watched the rest of the activity from the back of the ambulance, while the medics examined him. Not one hair of his body had been singed.

About an hour later, the fire marshal gave him a pair of rubber boots and told him he could go into the apartment. Don trudged through the filthy, soggy rooms, inspecting the damage of the fire, water and smoke. It seemed strange that in such a short period of time, familiar things could change so drastically. They had just made the last payment on their two-year-old furniture, and now it and everything else they owned was reduced to rubble. He felt exposed and defenseless.

The electric knife they had received as a wedding gift had been mounted on the wall. Now it was completely melted. The door-knob that Don had used to open the door just moments before the fire was extinguished was gone, too, the brass-coloured metal dripping down the door. He looked at his hand—surprised there were no signs of burns from the red-hot metal. He was even more surprised when a firefighter later told him that a special fire-retardant drywall had been used in the apartment. Because it doesn't allow heat to spread, it acts as an incinerator and significantly increases the intensity of the fire it contains.

While Don was still sleeping, the building superintendent and his two adult sons had mounted the stairs with a large fire extinguisher. When they opened the door of the apartment, the flames pushed them back with such force that they slammed the door closed immediately. "If someone's in there, it's too late now."

The marshal photographed the iron and ironing board, as Don surveyed the ruins. They walked into the bedroom. "Is this where you were?" Don nodded.

"You're a lucky man. From my twenty-five years of experience, I'd say you should have been carried out of here in a body bag!"

When money
speaks, the
truth is silent.
—Russian
proverb

07
Under the bridge

Later that morning, Don drove to the dental office in Westmount. He knew Monika would be devastated and he wanted to go in person to give her the news.

Monika knew, right when she saw him, that something was terribly wrong. He had dug through the rubble until he had found some pants and a shirt. But they were filthy and smelled like smoke. When he told her the news, she fell apart, convinced it was all her fault.

The fire marshal had found the iron in the "off" position. A faulty thermostat had caused the iron to overheat. But thousands of dollars of damage had been done, and unfortunately Don and Monika had no insurance. The building sued them to cover damages.

The next two weeks passed in a blur. The superintendent arranged to have a dumpster hauled up just outside their fourth-storey window and they rummaged through their possessions, tossing them out the window and shoveling out the debris—remains of their life—like ashes from a wood-burning stove.

They stayed with Don's parents while they looked for an apartment, and his grandmother—Granny Dalzell—who was living with his parents at the time, hugged them again and again, telling them how sorry she was. Friends and relatives collected money—more than a thousand dollars—and gave it to them.

On the Saturday after the fire, one of Don's cousins got married. His parents talked them into going, so they bought two new outfits and went. They felt as if they were in a strange, little world of their own—outsiders looking in on the happiness of others, unable to take part in it themselves. When they were there, they overheard someone talking about the fire: "Maybe God caused it, to teach them a lesson. He'll use it to steer them back to himself."

"If that's the kind of God they have," Don told Monika later, "I don't want any part of him. I'm through with God."

He figured they were on their own, now. If God took everything they owned, Don sure wasn't going to go to him, begging for help to get it back. They would have to find a way to make the money to get back on their feet.

The opportunity came sooner then they expected, and from an unlikely place. They were eating at the downtown restaurant two weeks after the fire, when B.J. Cameron came over to talk to them during his break. "How's the real estate business going?" He asked Don. "Been thinking about buying myself a house. Can you come over some time to talk?"

Don met with him a few days later, in his home. B.J. introduced him to Shelley, the woman he lived with, and her two teenage daughters.

"Don't worry about the price," he said, as he led him to the living room to talk. "'We just want to find the perfect house." Don was surprised. This guy, a waiter, was his first client to say money wasn't an issue. "I have a little business on the side that's going pretty well. Maybe it would interest you."

Ah, that explained it. A little business on the side? This sounded interesting. "Tell me about it," Don answered.

B.J. asked him if he knew people who liked nice cars. He said he could sell them to Don for a very reasonable price, and Don could resell them for a profit. Don said he'd think about it.

They met several more times. "These cars you're talking about—are they hot?" Don asked.

B.J.'s answer was allusive. "Not hot, Donny, just a little warm." Don knew, although he didn't quite admit it to himself, that there was no such thing. It was either cold (legal) or hot (illegal).

Don and Monika moved into a new apartment, this one closer to central Montreal. They needed to find a way to get back on their feet. This car business sounded like it had possibilities, but Don was cautious. He decided to start slowly, with just one vehicle. He had an old high-school friend named Gord, who worked at a small shop on Sherbrooke Street near McGill University. He was looking for a van for the business.

"Can you get me a van for a decent price?" Don asked B.J.

"I'll get you any car, any make, for $3,500. Registration in the buyer's name, license plate, keys, ownership and bill of sale from a well-known dealership—all included in the package."

Don paid the $3,500, cash, for a white van and sold it to his friend for $4,800. It was a good day's work.

Another man named Randy Hill, dark haired and forty-ish, worked for the downtown store. He loved cars and had been in the car business himself. When he heard about the deal on the van, he pumped Don for more information and said he might be interested in buying some more cars to sell to some of his contacts.

Within several weeks, Don bought a Jeep, a Volvo, a few Cadillacs and a Lincoln. The orders were processed through B.J. —Don described what Hill wanted. A few days later, the cars were ready to be picked up at a designated spot, after Don handed over the cash.

At first, Don planned to sell two or three cars, just enough to get them out of the hole they had found themselves in after the fire. But it was too easy—every car seemed easier than the one before. The business grew, and by Christmas Don was into it full-time. His real estate business was just a front for his other activities.

Don would get an order for a car, usually from Hill. He'd place the order with B.J., who would send spotters out to drive around until they found the right vehicle, usually at a dealership, but sometimes in a driveway in a wealthy neighbourhood. The spotters would bring the address back to B.J., who would send a thief to get the vehicle. The thief would hot-wire the car, or take it out for a test drive from a dealership and make a mould of the keys, then come back to steal the car later. Or, if it was the right dealership, he would pay an inside contact $100 for a set of keys.

B.J. had contacts who worked for the department of automobile registration for Quebec, who would process the paperwork for a fee, as well as people who would sell him a bill of sale from inside a dealership.

The car, with the paperwork in the glove compartment, would always be dropped off and picked up under the Jacques Cartier Bridge, the bridge that linked greater Montreal to the South Shore. It was easy to locate, even for someone not so familiar with the city. The street underneath it was lined with apartments on one side. The other side stretched out under the shadow of the huge, old bridge. It was the perfect spot.

B.J. and Don never stripped down stolen cars for parts. They were strictly in the resale business. They had some rules for themselves: Don't own a stolen car and never sell a car to someone who can't afford it. Their customers were doctors, lawyers, business owners and anyone else whose lifestyle could provide a front for the organization, by making the purchase of a luxury vehicle appear feasible.

Their other rule was never to do business over the phone. But they relaxed that rule a little, when B.J. fell off a curb and broke his leg. His hospital stay made him less mobile and more dependent on the telephone for communication.

The accident also marked a change in their relationship. When Don visited him in the hospital, B.J.'s attitude toward him changed subtly. He became more dependent on Don, recognizing that Don was capable of putting through more deals than the average person. Their alliance became less distant, less professional and more personal.

Most mornings, Don would drop Monika off at work, pick up a newspaper and drive to B.J.'s place. They would spend the day doing transactions.

One morning, he arrived to find Shelley in tears. "B.J.'s gone. He drove away mad last night and didn't come home." Don knew him well enough, by now, to have an idea where he might be. He drove past a nearby strip of cheap motels, until he spotted his car. Then he found a phone booth, looked up the number of the motel and called B.J.'s room.

He was still in bed and he wasn't alone. He was a carouser, and it didn't take much of a fight with Shelley to set him off. The same thing happened several times, but Don usually managed to track him down.

Once, B.J. took Don into the back streets of downtown Montreal to meet David Lachance. He worked for B.J., negotiating keys and bills of sale. His brother, Pierre, was lower on the organizational ladder—one of the thieves. But it wasn't until later that Don learned their names. B.J. stopped the car suddenly and said to Don, "Our man's coming up to the car, Don, and climbing into the back seat. You can talk to him, but to you he's just a voice. Don't ask his name and don't turn around. Don't even shift your body."

As Don got deeper into the organization, Monika's discomfort grew. One afternoon, they went with B.J. and Shelley to their cottage in Chelsea. They were lounging on chairs, enjoying the view, when Don noticed Monika watching B.J. closely, her eyes half closed. "B.J.," she said, suddenly breaking the silence, "what will happen if you guys get caught?'

"Get caught doing what?" B.J. answered, laughing. Everything was a joke to him.

Monika didn't laugh. "I don't know all that you guys are into, but I'm worried."

She *didn't* know all they were into. Just recently, they had been looking into shipping cars overseas. Randy Hill came from Great Britain and he had connections there. It looked as if there were some promising possibilities. There were also other opportunities, unconnected to the cars. They were getting a reputation for getting their hands on other highly-desirable objects, such as "fresh" credit cards, which they sold for $100.

"Don't worry, Monika. Don's not in too deep. We won't get caught, but if we do, it's me that's the criminal, not Don." He winked. "There's nothing they can pin on him—I'll be the fall guy."

B.J. sounded convincing. He was a good talker, all right. He was a recovering alcoholic, and he often invited Don to go to AA meetings to hear him speak. He stood there, in front of all those strangers, calm, composed, blue eyes shining behind his glasses. "My name is B.J. Cameron. I am an alcoholic…" *And a womanizer, and a criminal,* Don would add in his mind. He was a good speaker, though, and strangely enough, a good friend.

That night, on the way home from the cottage, Monika and Don argued about his involvement with Cameron. "You've been in long enough, Don. You should get out now."

He didn't even answer her, just gripped the steering wheel and kept his mouth shut. He wasn't in the mood for another argument. The tension between them had been building lately. There was so much Monika didn't understand. Once you made money like that so easily, you couldn't just walk away from it. He knew he couldn't go back now, probably never could.

It wasn't just the money, either. It was the challenge, the excitement of doing something daring. The day before, as Don was driving a stolen black sports car to the drop-off spot, a police cruiser had pulled up next to him. For a split second their eyes had locked. Don had looked at him steadily, even nodded a little, and then the light had changed and the cruiser moved ahead. It was a heady feeling, to know what he was getting away with, and it made him feel a surge of adrenaline.

He loved the city, especially at night. Things came alive and started moving, when the sun went down and the lights came up. Many of their transactions took place in strip bars. The music, the drinking, the carousing that went on there gave him a rush and helped him leave behind normal life that could get so stale.

The thing he liked best about the city was the anonymity of it.

When he drove through the streets and the alleys of Montreal, and under the Jacques Cartier Bridge, especially at night, he felt protected by the size of the city. He was faceless and nameless, and he was invincible.

Be sure your sin
will find you out.
−Numbers 32:23

08
Busted!

"Don Heron! Montreal police here." It was 5:30 A.M., the Friday morning before Mother's Day weekend, when the voice blasted through the speaker in the bedroom of Don and Monika's apartment. Don groped for the phone connected to the intercom, his body tensing at the word *police*.

Must be collecting for traffic tickets, he thought. But why would the police come to collect this early in the morning? *This is odd*, he thought. Ignoring the voice in the receiver, he drifted back to sleep.

The second time he was awakened, it was by a loud knock at the door. He tiptoed out of bed and looked through the peephole. The two men were civilian dressed, but he knew they were the cops he had heard over the intercom earlier. Don told himself he must be dreaming. He crawled back into bed with Monika, who slept soundly, undisturbed by all the activity.

But when he heard the sound of a key in the door, he knew this was no dream. For the first time that morning, he was wide awake. Every muscle in his body froze and a chill ran down his spine, as he lay there, pretending to be asleep, listening to footsteps approaching his bed.

"Don Heron?" the voice came from the foot of the bed. Slowly, against his will, Don opened his eyes and sat straight up. He saw the same two men, police badges held in their hands. Monika gasped as she sat up, clutching the sheets to cover herself. "God, what's going on here?"

"Ma'am, I'm Sergeant Dupont from the Montreal police and we have a warrant to search your premises. Get out of bed and get dressed, please." Don and Monika scrambled out of bed, as the officers watched. Monika asked them to leave while she dressed, but they refused, so she grabbed something out of the dresser and put it on.

The apartment was on ground level, with access to a patio through sliding doors. These doors were opened and two more officers, who had been stationed there to stop any escape attempt, stomped in.

Don's mind whirled, as Dupont led him to the dining room table and began shuffling through a folder of papers. "We're looking for stolen cars, automobile registration papers, auto parts, keys or anything else of that nature."

Although he couldn't bring himself to look at her, Don knew Monika was glaring at him—confused, angry, questioning. This is what she had feared for so long. She had begged him to get out of the business, but he had continued to assure her that his activities, though not legal, were nothing too serious, and he would never get caught. She was stunned by this sudden intrusion into their lives. Then it was his turn to be surprised when she requested, and was granted, permission to make a pot of tea.

He could see into the kitchen from where he sat. The officers were rummaging through cupboards, drawers, the stove and the refrigerator. *Close call! Glad I removed the cash—$12,000—hidden in the freezer.* It was payment for two stolen cars. By this time the price had gone up to $6,000 per car. The policemen moved into the bathroom, where they took the top off the toilet tank and looked into the water. In the bedroom, they rummaged through the pockets of pants and coats. When they were finished, they had found a set of Cadillac keys that were eventually linked to a stolen car. Don continued to insist that this was all a mistake.

Dupont looked doubtful. Then abruptly he said, "Maybe you're right. We may have busted the wrong person. Let's call into headquarters and check things out." He dialed the number and handed the receiver to Don, explaining that they needed identification. The voice on the other end was kind and apologetic. "If you could give us your name, social insurance number and date of birth, maybe we can get this all straightened out for you, sir." Don eagerly identified himself.

Dupont told Monika she was free to go to work. Her hands shook as she buttoned up her white uniform, but she calmly kissed Don goodbye and walked out the door. The sun was shining as she walked to the bus stop and took the city bus to the dental office.

No sooner had she gone, though, than two uniformed officers came into the apartment and handcuffed Don, and then led him out into the hallway. Word of the police raid had spread through the building, and a small crowd of their neighbours had gathered in the main entrance. There was a murmur of shocked, excited whispers, as the crowd parted and Don passed through, hemmed in by officers.

Don was perplexed by the polite treatment he had received all morning. He didn't know then, that the officers had been watching him, photographing him, following him and listening in on his phone conversations for eight months. They had rented an apartment overlooking the drop-off spot under the Jacques Cartier Bridge, where they had photographed dozens of transactions. They told him later, they knew him better than he knew himself—intimate details about his background, his family life and his personality— knew him well enough to feel certain they could arrest him and bring him in without any problems. When they asked him to identify himself over the phone to headquarters, it was simply to match his

Stolen luxury car rings broken with 13 arrests

Police have arrested 13 people, seized more than $500,000 worth of deluxe cars and broken three major auto theft rings in Montreal with connections in the United States and Europe.

The 11 men and two women were arrested following 23 police raids Thursday in Montreal, the South Shore and Laval. They are to face hundreds of charges in court.

"The ring consisted of thieves and distributors, and they didn't touch anything worth less than $20,000," said Const. Norman Couillard of the Montreal Urban Community police.

He said dozens, perhaps hundreds, of Montrealers are driving around in stolen cars and don't know it.

The Cadillacs, Corvettes, Lincolns and other deluxe cars were sold for $6,000 to $12,000 each.

"People in possession of these cars, and who don't know they're stolen, probably think they got a good deal," said Couillard.

Most of the cars were stolen in the Montreal area. While some were sold in Montreal and other parts of Quebec, others have been seized in Ontario, the U.S. (especially Miami), Lebanon and Luxembourg.

"The ring is connected to other major auto theft rings operating in other countries," said Couillard.

The arrests follow months of investigation by MUC Det.-Sgts. Normand Desrochiers and Gabriel Morin of the auto theft squad.

Police are asking people who believe they may be in possession of a stolen car to contact the auto theft squad at 934-2194.

"It may sound strange to ask people to turn in their cars, but I must stress that more seizures are going to be made in near future," said Couillard.

"It's preferable to getting stopped on the highway, on the way for a summer vacation and us maybe seizing the car then."

Article about the arrests in Montreal's The Gazette, May 8, 1982

voice with the voice they had recorded from hours of bugged phone conversations.

But Don's treatment was very different from that of others in the auto-theft ring, who were arrested at the very same time. He learned later that Cameron was picked up by a special task force at his Chelsea cottage. These men had special training and were assigned to high-risk cases. Cameron's door was smashed in and he

Démantèlement de 3 réseaux de voleurs d'autos de luxe

■ La police de la CUM a procédé dans la journée de jeudi à 23 perquisitions et 13 arrestations: 11 hommes, 2 femmes, en rapport avec 3 réseaux d'autos volées qui opéraient pour la plupart dans la région de Montréal mais aussi en Ontario, aux États-Unis ainsi qu'en Europe (Luxembourg et Liban). Cette opération dure depuis quelques mois. Ce sont des voitures de luxe qui étaient évaluées de $20,000 et plus. Le tout s'élève à plus d'un demi-million de dollars. Ces voitures étaient revendues entre $6,000 à $12,000. D'autres perquisitions vont être effectuées prochainement et la police demande aux citoyens s'ils ont des doutes sur la provenance de leur auto de communiquer avec le lieutenant détective Michel Doré à 934-2194.

Cette opération fut menée par les sergents détectives Normand Desrochers et Gabriel Morin sous les ordres du Lieutenant Michel Doré.

Article in Montreal's La Presse, May 8, 1982

was dragged from his bed and pinned between the refrigerator and stove while he was handcuffed.

Just before they left the apartment, one of the officers took the sunglasses from Don's pocket and threw them onto the ironing board. He winked at his partner. "Where you're going," he said to Don, "you won't be needing those." As they escorted him down the hall and out of the building, one of them took Don's keys and checked his empty mailbox.

Don sat in the back seat of the cruiser, hands cuffed behind him, and listened to the officers talk about their weekend plans. "I guess you won't need to make any plans," one of them yelled over his shoulder, laughing. "Nope. My guess is you won't need plans for the next twelve years." Don didn't say a word, but his face grew pale.

He had a strange condition—he was never sure if it was medical or just an escape mechanism—that caused him, during his most stressful moments, to fall asleep. Just when the officers were thoroughly enjoying their jokes about Don's future behind bars and revelling in the thought of how miserable he must be feeling in the back seat, he leaned against the window and fell asleep. When they glanced back and saw him sleeping, they abruptly stopped laughing. They woke him up when they reached the jail.

Don was taken into a receiving area and photographed, then fingerprinted. An officer emptied his pockets, and the contents were put into a brown paper bag. He was marched down a long corridor. As he walked, he noticed smaller halls extending from his, each dim and cut off by bars. Then he was put behind his own bars in his own cell, where he waited, his body rigid, his mind numb.

09
Monika

Monika sat in the back of the bus on the way to the dental office. She pressed her cheek hard against the moist window and watched the houses, the street signs, the office buildings go by. Everything was the same as it had been the day before—she even recognized the same faces at the bus stop. *Probably thinking about the sitcom they watched on TV, or the steak thawing on the counter at home for tonight's barbecue*, she thought. It seemed like years since yesterday, since she had thought normal thoughts, like the two men in the seat ahead, who were arguing over where to buy tires.

She ignored the skinny woman with long brown hair who sat down next to her and said what a nice day it was. *A nice day?!* That was a funny thought. She wondered if Don was having a nice day back in the plush apartment they had both been so proud of. What kind of money had gotten them that apartment? What kind of mess had he gotten himself, gotten *them*, into? She cursed Don silently, as she thought about him back there with the police. Great looking with his baby face, brown hair and blue, laughing eyes; eyes that crinkled up in the corners. Full of confidence—too much confidence, maybe. Even cockiness. Yet it was that very thing that had drawn her to him all those years ago.

She had heard him tell the story of their first meeting so many times. She argued with him, saying it didn't really happen like that, but he stuck with his story. It was one of his favourites. He laughed at the same places each time he told it, and he always gave her that secret smile that said, *You know this is the way it happened, Moon. Come on, honey, just admit it. Or at least play along…* Now she replayed the story again in her mind.

They had met in first grade, and even then he had been funny and smart and always the first to take a dare.

Monika, tiny, with blonde hair cut just below the ears, almost never talked at school. This was partly because she was shy and partly because she didn't know a lot of English. Her parents had immigrated to Canada from Germany before she was born and her dad worked at the Noranda mines. They spoke German at home.

She watched Donny a long time before she gathered the courage to tell him she liked him. Even then, she didn't tell him, but her friend Christina did. It was in grade-one art class.

Don liked art, because he could talk out loud to the boy next to him and sometimes walk around the room a little while before the teacher noticed and told him to sit down. He was cutting a circle out of purple construction paper, when Christina came up behind him and whispered in his ear.

"Which girl do you like?" She pointed to a group of girls in the corner, giggling over their scissors and glue. Then, she lowered her voice even more and said very earnestly, "You better like Monika Serafinowicz, because she likes you."

Donny dropped his scissors on the floor and turned red. Then he held up his purple circle, so that the others would think he was admiring it, and with one eye, he peeked over the rim of the paper at Monika. She knew he liked her, too.

A few years later, she found out he had a wonderful sister named

Janice, and the two girls became best friends. Once, while they were whispering together in the big German feather bed at Monika's house, the girls made a pact. They would always be best friends, and someday they would be even more than that. When Monika was old enough, she would marry Don, so that they could be real sisters for the rest of their lives.

One tear squeezed its way out of Monika's eye and down her cheek, but she brushed it away and every muscle on her face tightened as she pushed the next one back in. She looked down at her knuckles, small and white and hard against the bar of the seat ahead, and she cursed Don again, and then God, and even the men still arguing over the tires.

Two things
never live up
to their
advertising
claims:
the circus
and sin.
—unknown

10
Trapped

In the dark cell just across from his, Don could see Randy Hill, arrested at the same time. For a split second, their eyes met. Then they looked away. They were smart enough not to give any sign that they knew each other. But even without looking, Don could sense Hill's frustration. He paced back and forth, back and forth in his tiny cell. It made Don nervous. This was a guy who had everything—his own business, an expensive house in the best part of the city, a wife and two daughters. And here he was now, pacing like an animal trapped in a cage.

In his own cell, Don began negotiations with God. *If you'll just get me out of this mess,* he told God, *I'll straighten my life up—you'll see. I'll get away from these guys who got me into this stuff and I'll*—a guard banged on Don's door and offered him a cigarette. He jumped up—nothing sounded better than a good smoke right now. But then, abruptly, he changed his mind and refused the cigarette.

He looked up. *There, you see, God, I told you I'm a changed man. I'll never smoke again, if you'll just get me out of here.*

He spent the rest of the morning trying to make deals with God, but he had the feeling his prayers weren't getting any higher than the ceiling.

The picture of Monika, as he had last seen her, drifted into his mind. He couldn't believe she had made a pot of tea. She had looked calm and she was as beautiful as ever, but her quiet smile was gone and he had seen her hands shake as she stirred her tea. She'd be at work by now…. "Guard, I have to call my wife. Can I use the phone?" he yelled at the guard who came around with a cheese sandwich, but the guard just looked at Don and shook his head. Don looked at the dried-up sandwich, moaned and tossed it into the toilet. The flush, as it went down, echoed through the nearly empty corridors. "What about a lawyer? I need to call my lawyer!" He yelled at the guard's receding back.

The jerk! He thought as he threw himself down onto the metal bed. *The stupid, cocky jerk. They're all jerks—every one of them.* This included the whole system—the justice system and law enforcement and of course everyone who had gotten him into this mess to begin with. Even his parents… What about his parents? He wanted to blame them; wanted to pin this mess on their shoulders. Wasn't everyone really just a victim of his past? The "sins of their fathers" thing? There must be some way that the whole thing was their fault, even if he couldn't explain exactly how or why. But this was a lie, and he knew it.

He gripped the bars of his cell, shaking them in his frustration. "What am I doing in this hell?" he thought. Then he turned away from the bars, and letting out a deep breath, he stretched out on the cot against the back wall. His thoughts kept returning to his parents and his idyllic childhood. "How did I get from there to here?" He asked sleepily.

His thoughts became disconnected and slowly, involuntarily, he began to drift in and out of sleep. His mind moved backward, back before he got into this mess, before he met Cameron, before his undercover assignments, before he married Monika, back, even before he met Monika…*The little dog called Petit Loup. Fishing with Dad. Dad's TV show. Dad and Mom looking at him, laughing. Then surprised and crying, but with such love. Such incredible love. Building a camp up north together. Snowmobiles and snow. Always lots and lots of snow.*

When I approach a child, he inspires in me two sentiments: tenderness for what he is, and respect for what he may become.
—Louis Pasteur

11

Donny

One of his earliest memories was of a snow-covered rink on a cold, clear day in mid winter. He was three years old. "Ouch!" He yelled as he picked himself up and tried to take another step before he fell again. It was his first time ice-skating. At the beginning, he had been excited, but now he was getting mad. Each time he tried to move, he fell. He refused to give up though, so he tried again, and again and again. And then, sitting there on the ice, brushing the snow away, he noticed something strange and surprising, too.... "Hey, Mom, no wonder I keep falling—there's ice on this rink!"

It has been said that Canada is "six months of hockey and three months of bad ice." For Don, growing up in northern Quebec meant sliding, snowshoeing, snowmobiling and, of course, hockey. But summer did come every year, even if it was a little late—rarely did the snow melt before May, or the ice on the lake thaw before June. And when winter relented, Don was ready with his fishing rod, to embark on his favourite sport of all.

By the time he was old enough to talk, his dad's widely publicized arrest and imprisonment in the late 1940s (for preaching on the streets of Rouyn) had nearly disappeared from the short-term memory of the public. Evangelical Protestants in Quebec, though still small in number, were no longer so opposed by the largely Catholic majority. The fierce opposition to his father's preaching had mellowed and he was the respected pastor of the Baptist church in Rouyn-Noranda. He was also the host of *Sur les ailes de la foi* (On Wings of Faith), a half-hour television program which aired during prime time on Saturday nights on CKRN-TV.

Don's mother, Georgia Dalzell Heron, was a miner's daughter. She had left her job as a nurse to marry Murray and start a family. Don was the middle child, sandwiched between two older sisters, Susan and Joanne, and two younger sisters, Janice and Carolyn. They had a dog named Petit Loup, or Little Wolf, and a cat, and sometimes—though never all at once—a guinea pig, a bird and a fish. Their house was on the corner and close to the big hill where they went snowmobiling and sliding in the winter.

His parents had told him, ever since he could remember, about God's love for him. And his dad also told him about sin. He figured out that when he picked a fight with Janice, or slipped out the back door to play street hockey with his friends when his mom said to clean his room, he was sinning. He figured he needed Jesus, just like all those people his dad was preaching to in church meetings and on his TV show. So Don made a sincere commitment to follow Jesus, when he was six years old.

The church bought some land thirty miles north—way back in the bush—and began to build a summer youth camp on the edge of a large lake with icy-cold water. They named the camp after the lake—Opasatica. First they cleared out trees to build a road. Then they cleared away the space they needed and began to build cabins and a dining hall. Every summer they worked there, and some-times even on weekends during the school year. By the time they were finished, they had six or seven cabins, a dining hall, a chapel and a waterfront dock with boats. Don loved every minute at the camp. He built, repaired, cut brush and daydreamed about the day he would be old enough to drive the pickup truck around.

One year, the new chapel they built burnt to the ground. Another time, during an especially hard winter, he and his dad headed for the camp to check things out. For an hour and a half they trudged deep into the bush on snowshoes. When they arrived and got the first glimpse of the dining hall through the trees, Don moaned.

The building had collapsed—the roof had caved in under the weight of piles and piles of snow. Dismayed, he looked at his dad. His father stood silent, as still and sturdy as the tall, dark trees that surrounded him in the cold, white snow. After a moment, he nodded. "Yep, we'll have lots of work to do this spring."

One night his parents' friend Arnold Boulianne was visiting for supper. Between bites of Don's mom's mashed potatoes, Arnold told the kids about a trip he had taken with their dad.

"We were in the car on a dark night and the worst thunderstorm you've ever seen hit. The rain was coming down so hard we couldn't see a foot ahead. Then the storm got worse. I started complaining, but not for long, because something your dad said shut me up..." He paused to take a bite.

Don couldn't wait. "Well, what was it? What did my dad say?"

"'There's one thing we should praise God for,' he said. I thought about it for a while, but, for the life of me, I couldn't think of what there was to praise God for in that miserable storm. But I was curious. 'What's that?' I asked. 'Let's be thankful for the windshield,' your dad answered. I started laughing, then, and the storm didn't seem so bad."

Lots of people had stories to tell about his father, and Don had never grown tired of hearing them. And he had never stopped watching his dad. He had even thought that maybe someday he would like to be a preacher, too.

Govern your
passions, or
they will
govern you.
−Latin proverb

12
The rush

Don stirred in his sleep and woke up to see the guard peering at him. The sight jerked him back to a reality as cold and hard as the steel bars that closed him in. He lay where he was and stared at the ceiling, following the pattern of dots with his eyes—tracing them across the stained tiles. It occurred to him that he had not moved from there to here—from preacher's kid to accused criminal—with one grand leap. He had inched his way here. He had traversed the huge chasm between then and now one tiny step, one little dot, at a time.

He drifted into that state again—the same half-dreaming, half-probing images. This time his thoughts turned toward his teenage years, and he heard the angry voice of Monika.

"What is it about doing these crazy things that gives you such a rush?" Monika and Don were fifteen. She was mad at Don, again, and they were fighting. She lived close by, and by now, their childhood crush had grown into something more serious. Janice and Monika had remained best friends. Don and David Foster, his best friend, and the two girls spent hours hanging out together. Sometimes it bugged Janice that Monika was so wrapped up in her brother, and it bugged Don that Janice had to tell Monika every little thing he did.

That's why they were fighting now. That morning, he had taken Janice for a snowmobile ride. Things had seemed a little slow so he had sped them up. Pushing the throttle all the way down, he had blasted, full throttle, into a group of guys on the street. Janice had screamed and he had laughed, yelling, "They'll move!" And they had, of course, but just in time. They had cursed him, as he roared away, snow flying, and Janice had fumed all the way home.

That winter, like every year between Christmas and New Year's, David invited Don to his parents' cottage. It was up north on a lake, remote, and with no phone lines or roads leading up to it, completely isolated. The only way to get there was by boat in the summer and by snowmobile in the winter. That's what they loved about it.

This year, they planned to go with David's cousin, Jerry, and another friend named Mike. David and Jerry managed to get away sooner than Don and Mike, so they went up to the cottage early. Don and Mike had planned to join them in two days, but they found they could go sooner, and since they had no way of contacting the guys who were already there, they came up with a great practical joke.

They planned to sneak up on the cottage and pretend to steal David and Jerry's snowmobile. Mike, who said he knew how to hot-wire the vehicle, would drive away with it, while Don, who had a frighteningly real-looking pellet gun, would "hold up" David and Jerry.

Don and Mike arrived at the cottage in the middle of a frigid, starless night, two days before the two guys already there were expecting them. They walked the last half mile, wearing ski masks, so they could sneak up on their friends. When Mike went to the snowmobile to start it up, David and Jerry heard the noise and looked outside the door to check it out. Don pointed his gun at them and yelled, disguising his voice. "Get back in the cottage or I'll shoot!"

David and Jerry ran back in and slammed the door, convinced that they were being robbed by hardened criminals. Things weren't going as planned, however, because Mike couldn't get the snowmobile started. Don kept screaming at the guys inside, just to shake them up a little. But he had forgotten that Jerry had military training.

Inside the cottage, Jerry found his uncle's gun. "Stay low," he whispered to David, and began looking for ammunition. When he spotted it, he groaned. It was on a shelf, just above the window. He knew he shouldn't reach for it, and put himself within the line of fire. So he and David waited there on the floor, watching the door, unable to load the shotgun.

"Open the door, or I'll smash it down and kill you!" Don yelled. Jerry opened it, and looked up into the barrel of Don's gun. Don made them lie on the floor, face down, and said to Mike, "Let's kill them or they'll identify us." Then Don and Mike, still disguised by ski masks, paced back and forth between the two trembling victims on the floor and discussed all the possible ways they could deal with them.

But five minutes of this was too much. Don's voice cracked and he fell to the floor, laughing until he cried. Mike laughed with him and Jerry smiled weakly, but David lay there, as white as a sheet. Suddenly, he jumped up and started punching Don. It took all three guys to hold him back, and then he collapsed to the floor and began to cry like a baby.

Don looked down at the pellet gun in his hand, surprised that this thing could make his tough friend cry.

By the time he was eighteen and had had his driver's license for two years, he had lost count of his accidents and "close calls." He was out of control, and he knew it. He loved the sudden rush when there was danger involved—when he was taking a risk. He began to live for that rush, and it came to mean more to him then anything else, including, though he never would admit it, even to himself, the faith his parents had tried so hard to pass down to him.

Don knew that he was hurting his parents. The thought made him feel guilty. He didn't want to hurt them—there was nothing planned or calculated about all the stupid things he did.

Janice often said, "Donny, when you're around, things happen." They weren't always bad things, either. Just always exciting things. Sometimes he felt as if he was sitting on a volcano—and a huge explosion could happen any time. He loved that feeling. Everyone else got so uptight about everything. But not Don. Even the thought of death didn't scare him. He told people he knew he wouldn't live to be twenty-one. They were shocked and told him not to say that kind of thing.

After high school, Don and Monika left home in Rouyn-Noranda to attend Cambrian College in Sudbury, Ontario. It was their first taste of independence and they made the most of it. Don's thirst for excitement and his curiosity to try new things had steadily grown. It was during his college years that the pangs of guilt that had once been so strong, came less and less often. What was life, anyway, if it wasn't to be enjoyed?

He studied law and security administration, and boarded with a family next door to the place where Monika was boarding.

That summer Don went back home to work at the Noranda mines. Monika stayed in Sudbury, where she began working as an apprentice hairdresser. Then she fell for another guy, and broke up with Don.

When he returned to college that fall, he hit the party scene with new energy. He moved in with his old friend David, who was in the same program at school. They seemed to be competing against each other, to see who could party hardest. Don wanted to forget about Monika. Drinking and partying seemed to help.

Then at Christmas time, Monika broke up with her boyfriend and she and Don got back together.

Every sin is
the result of a
collaboration.
—Stephen King

13
Wake-up call

Don woke up and shook his head, trying to clear his mind. He looked at his watch—nearly 10 P.M. He had been sleeping—a broken, troubled sleep—for hours.

The memories had played before his eyes like one of those silent movies from the twenties. Now, he was in the real world again, but all he wanted to do was to escape, to shut his eyes and go back to sleep—this time, a dreamless sleep. He felt trapped and scared. But he felt something more. For the first time that he could remember, a dark cloud of doubt had crept in. Doubt in himself and all the decisions he had made to get himself and Monika into this situation.

He tried to picture Monika, and wondered what she must be doing. She would have finished work hours ago. Had she tried to track him down? He was sure she must have contacted Janice—they had kept their pact and remained best friends. Had they told his parents about the arrest? He hoped not. Somehow, he couldn't bear for them to know.

"Heron, come with us." His thoughts were interrupted by two men. One was nondescript, with an average build. The other was huge and carried a cane. He slapped the cane against his meaty hand a few times and said, laughing, "Hopefully, I won't have to use this."

After they unlocked his cell, they took him in an elevator, separated in the middle by bars, to the first floor. They led him into an interrogation room. The big guy spoke right away. "Well, Heron, at least you don't have to be lonely—all your friends are here with you."

Don answered quietly, keeping his voice emotionless and his face a mask without expression. "I don't know what you're talking about."

"B.J. Cameron, Randy Hill, David Lachance, Pierre Lachance. Ever heard those names before? They're all here, Heron, and we know everything." Don looked straight ahead, and the big guy left the room. The other one now spoke for the first time. "You messed around with the wrong guys, kid, and now you're in a heck of a mess, yourself."

The big guy returned carrying a box full of files. Without saying a word, he began to pull them out, one by one. Typed telephone conversations between him and Cameron. Photos of stolen cars delivered under the bridge. Photos of large sums of money changing hands. Photos of Don with Hill. Photos of Don with Cameron.

"Funny that you don't know these men. You look pretty friendly to me." Don could feel the mask that was his face crumble away under the gaze of the two officers. But he still didn't answer.

"We've been on to you for eight months. We've got more evidence against you than we've had on any other auto-theft ring in the history of this province, and this one's the biggest." It was then that he told Don about their stakeout apartment across from the bridge, twenty-four hours a day, and bugging his phone. Don had incriminated himself when he had inadvertently given them the voice match over the phone earlier in the day. "The way we see it, you and Cameron are at the top of the organization. Cameron

70

already signed a confession. Now it's your turn." He held out a pen and Don stared at it. "You sign, you get out of here, back home to your lovely wife."

They know everything, Don thought. *The sooner I get out, the sooner I can get a lawyer and get help. Monika must be worried sick. Cameron already confessed.* Hesitantly, he took the pen and signed. Then he went over every piece of evidence with them—identified every car, every transaction and every face he knew.

It was after midnight when the police took him home.

His sister Janice was at the apartment. She was lying on the couch, and Monika was ironing clothes. Janice barely spoke to him—just gave him a long look, hugged Monika and walked out the door.

They didn't fight that night, as he'd thought they would. Monika just said, "I knew this would happen. Now what?"

"I'm okay—protected." Even he didn't believe what he was saying. His voice sounded hollow, insecure. "It's B.J. who's in trouble."

That night seemed agonizingly long to Don. As he lay there, he heard Monika's soft, regular breathing. He was glad she could sleep. He didn't know she had used Valium—taken from the dental office—to calm her nerves.

He thought how hard it was going to be to conceal this from his family. He couldn't stand the thought of their knowing—his parents, especially, and Granny Dalzell. What would they think, if they found out about his arrest? But eventually they would have to know. He was still awake the next morning, as the first rays of sunlight crept into the room. Even with the light, his future, like a rain cloud, hung over him, dark and ominous.

The next morning Don and B.J. met with a lawyer named Ronald Savage. They drove a rented car, since both of their cars had been impounded. Mr. Savage took them from his office into the parking lot for the meeting because, he said, they didn't need the complication of someone overhearing their conversation. Then he said that these would be serious charges and that they might want to consider paying off a judge in exchange for lesser time. "This will all be discussed in the future."

14
The last call

Maybe it was that cloud, that element of desperation that entered their lives on the day Don was arrested. Or maybe it was guilt over keeping the news from his parents. But four weeks after the arrest, Don said yes to his parents' invitation to the city-wide French evangelistic crusade. He regretted it by the time he ended the conversation and hung up the receiver.

Monika seemed oddly willing to go, and Don was surprised. His parents had invited them to this kind of thing before, and they had always managed to find excuses not to go. Too late for that now. This time they would go and make the best of it.

The choir was singing, as they arrived. Don strained to see past the people in the row ahead and scan the faces of the choir members—his mom had told him that one of his cousins was singing.

It was strange, sitting there. It was so much like church. There was a time when he had loved to go to church, but it seemed like so long ago, now.

He stood up mechanically when everyone got up to sing. He stared at the words of the song on the program he and Monika shared. She was singing softly, along with everyone else. He gripped the paper hard, his knuckles showing white. His lips pressed against each other so firmly that they formed one pale pink line. He felt like, if he had vocal chords, they were tied up into a little knot in the pit of his stomach. How could people sing? He wondered. For him it was a physical impossibility.

But he remembered singing when he was a kid. His mind shot back to all the times he had sung on his dad's TV show or at the street meetings. He had even played the guitar for a while. He had loved those meetings. His dad was the best storyteller he had ever heard. When he spoke, people listened. His dad explained so clearly, so simply, what the Bible said about the love of God. And always, when he got near to the end of his message, his voice would change. He would become less a preacher and more like a friend, speaking directly to each person who was listening.

"*God saw we were in trouble,*" he could hear his dad saying. "*God knew that each of us would choose to go our own way—a way of sin and pain. But he provided a path back to himself, one that would lead to happiness for us. A way by which we, no matter what we have done, could be forgiven. That's why Jesus came and died on the cross—to bridge that huge gap between us and God. But we have to believe and confess our need for him. That's faith. Is anyone here ready to take that step?*"

Don had taken that step when he was a kid, and so had Monika. She and Janice had knelt together on the high-school stage and hidden behind the red velvet curtain, as Monika had asked Jesus into her heart. From then on, she went to church every Sunday with the Herons.

When Don was fourteen, his dad baptized him in the lake at Camp Opasatica. It was an exhilarating moment, and as he came up out of the water, its icy coldness running down his back and sending goosebumps all over his body, he was sure he would do wonderful things for God, just like his dad. So what went wrong?

Why the great gap between the zealous ideals of a fourteen-year-old boy and the bitter cynicism of this twenty-four-year-old, standing frozen, with a tight knot in his gut? He tried to trace his life from that day to this, tried to find the thread, to understand how he had gotten where he was today—with the impending cloudburst—but it was a difficult thing to do.

He was sure there was never one great moment when he had thrown Christianity out the window. It was hundreds of little decisions, one tiny step at a time, that had taken him down this path. Losing his temper, choosing the wrong friends, thirsting for excitement at any cost, drinking with his buddies, partying with the union guys, doing "business" with B.J., ignoring Monika's warnings. Selfishness. Greed. Pride. Lust. The sum total of all the things that he had done, and all the things he was, was this bitter, scared person gripping the song sheet with the words he couldn't sing. All the wrong motivations and the wrong decisions, seemingly harmless at the time, had caused him, finally and completely, to turn his back on God. He saw it clearly now, but he was beyond the point of no return. He sat down, along with the others, when the song was over.

A hockey player from the Pittsburgh Penguins was invited to the front to speak. He was young and sincere, and as he spoke, Don listened. For a few minutes, his mind stopped wandering. Then the main speaker began his message. He wasn't what Don had expected, at all. He had a well-developed picture of evangelists. Big smile, with big white teeth. Slick, expensive suit. Lots of words, spilling out quickly—each sentence hurling forward faster than the one before. Loud, too, with lots of yelling and thumping.

Jacques Marcoux wasn't like that, at all. His talk was simple, not at all emotional, and full of facts. Don liked him, felt that he was dealing plainly. Still, he couldn't concentrate on the words. It was as if the cloud had descended lower and was so dark and heavy he could almost reach up and touch it. He was holding his breath, waiting for it to burst and a terrible thunderstorm to be unleashed. First, the charges would come down, then the trial, then his prison sentence. When that happened, his whole fragile existence would be shattered. He hated to think about others who would come down with him—his parents, his sisters, his grandparents, and Monika, of course. What would they all do when the cloud finally burst?

He was worried about a prison term. The words of the police officer who had tossed away his sunglasses played on his mind like a broken record: "Where you're going, you won't be needing these." And then, "Twelve years is what you'll get."

His thoughts were cut short by the speaker. "Do you have any concept of eternity? Any idea of how long forever is, compared to the moment that is your life? A little bird flies over the Atlantic Ocean, picks up a drop of water in his beak and carries it to the Pacific Ocean. Then he flies back to the Atlantic and picks up another drop, and makes the trip again and again, until he has emptied the whole Atlantic Ocean. That is just the beginning of eternity."

The idea made Don's mind whirl. If all of life was just a moment, what was a prison term? Things must look completely different from God's point of view, if he existed. What would it be like, to have that perspective? To see life, and all that happened in life, as only a part of a huge whole. It was as if Don had been blind, but suddenly he saw things he had never seen before. He wondered about the things he had been living for. What was money, really? Or the excitement he thrived on? Maybe they were distractions, to keep him from thinking bigger—thinking of reality. Maybe they were worse than distractions. Maybe they were deadly.

But he looked around at these people. He saw a lady with big hair, smiling smugly, head cocked a little to one side, her heavy perfume filling the air around her. And he said to himself, *I'm not going back. They'll want me in church three times a week and I can't do it. I can't go back now—it's too late.*

The preacher sat down and the choir started singing again. The words they sang stopped him in his tracks and sent him reeling.

> *Tu peux naître de nouveau (you can be born again),*
> *Tu peux tout recommencer (you can start all over again),*
> *Balayer ta vie passée (sweep away your old life).*
> *Et repartir à zéro (and start again at zero),*
> *Avec Jésus pour berger (with Jesus as your shepherd).*

At that moment he stopped struggling with his past. When had he begun to mess things up? At sixteen, maybe? Maybe earlier. But the fact was, he had taken his life into his own hands and he had thoroughly blown it. He couldn't go back to where he had left off at sixteen. He had to start all over at the beginning. Maybe he could give God another chance; or was it that maybe God would give him another chance?

"Going forward," walking up the aisle to pray with someone, wasn't really an emotional thing for him. He still felt frozen inside, and the cloud was still there hanging over him, threatening to explode. But he knew that if he could take this step, he could somehow face the explosion a little easier. A quote popped into his mind, something he had read on a plaque at the Alcoholics Anonymous meetings he had often visited with B.J. Cameron. *God grant me the serenity to accept the things I cannot change, the courage to change the things I can, and the wisdom to know the difference.*

Maybe he couldn't change his past or his prison term, but he sure as heck could change his life. He had to give it a try. He stepped out into the aisle, and Monika went with him.

Funny that he associated that plaque, that quote, with B.J. Cameron. There wasn't much serenity, courage or wisdom about B.J.'s life, and he was in as big a mess as Don, now. Those qualities made him think of someone else. They made him think of the camp chapel burning down, and a voice saying, "Son, when our work is done and it seems there's nothing else we can do—that's when things really get exciting. That's when God can take over, and act." They made him think of his father.

Don's dad was standing there weeping—Don and Monika saw him just as they were leaving. Don stood still and looked at him. Was it deep pain or deep joy that sent the tears, as if from a fountain, pouring out of his father's eyes and flowing down his cheeks? There was a verse he had taught Don years ago. *There is rejoicing in the presence of the angels of God over one sinner who repents.*

Don walked out of the building, lit a cigarette, and looked up at the sky. "God," he said, "I've shut you out. Now I'm letting you come in. I don't feel any different. I know you're there, now please show me."

Let us keep our
mouths shut
and our pens
dry, until we
know the facts.
−Anton J.
Carlson

15

A crack in the door

"How do you feel now?" It was the first thing Monika asked when they woke up the next morning.

"I've got a rotten headache."

"That's not what I meant."

Don was silent as he thought about her question. He had heard story after story of God's working overnight in people's lives. There's a man whose whole life is in shambles—a drunk, a bum, a criminal, maybe; and then the transformation takes place. He wakes up a new person, with a bright, permanent smile on his joyful face. He trades in his jeans and leather jacket for a suit, and he begins carrying a big Bible everywhere he goes (a bit like Daniel at the factory). He gives up every bad habit without a struggle, and his friends hardly recognize him as the same person. It was supposed to be that way. Didn't the Bible say something about someone turning to God and becoming a new person?

In the bathroom, as he splashed cold water on his face, he stared into the mirror. If he had expected to see a new man, he was disappointed. He looked the same, and worse than that, he still felt hard and a little cynical toward Christianity.

The next weeks were like that. No fanfare, no grandstand parade. He didn't stop going to bars and start going to church, instead. It wasn't until later that he recognized the significance of the night of the crusade in his life.

He was only aware of a subtle difference in his attitude, an opening of a closed door—just a crack. It was as if he had been walking, or running, in the opposite direction from God, and on that night he stopped, turned around and stood still. Any movement toward God was barely perceptible. But at least he was no longer running away. Just standing there, still and quiet, and a little worried. Looking at God. Waiting to see what would happen.

He didn't wait long. Just three weeks after the crusade, Don saw God's undeniable work in the circumstances of his life.

Since the arrest, he and Monika had felt a growing need to get away from Montreal. He talked with B.J. Cameron occasionally, enough to learn that he was on to new "projects." One of Don's high-school friends, Gord, who had bought the very first van from Don, had also bought a sports car for himself. But the latter transaction had occurred about the same time as the arrests, and his new car was seized by the police before he paid for it. Now the money was outstanding and the car was gone. One morning, two guys from the auto-theft ring showed up at Gord's workplace with a sawed-off shotgun to collect the $6,000 Gord hadn't paid. Gord went to the bank with the two men and withdrew $500. They explained that the $500 would cover the interest for today, but they would be back tomorrow for the $6,000 still owed. Gord went into hiding and Don helped him negotiate a deal with Cameron that cost Gord his pride and joy, a 1966 restored Jaguar.

Don wanted to get away from his old friends and all the associations he had with his life in the city, to begin again. But it was a hard time to find employment.

Monika picked him up in the car one day and surprised him with good news. "Your Uncle Lloyd called and said there's a job waiting for you in Windsor." None of the family, except Janice, knew of the arrest. But he had told them he was looking for work. Word had gotten to Susan, his oldest sister, who lived in Windsor with her family, and to their Uncle Lloyd, who worked for Ford Motors in Detroit. Uncle Lloyd had a friend named Hewie, who was a director in the Windsor company where Mike, Susan's husband, worked.

Occasionally, Hewie would stop into Lloyd's office at Ford for a quick cup of coffee and an exchange of news. It occurred to Lloyd, when he heard that Don needed a job, that maybe Hewie would have something for him at the Windsor company. But he hadn't seen him in months. He sat in his office and as he tapped his pen against his desk, he prayed about it: "Lord, if you want me to ask Hewie about a job for Don, have him come into my office."

His eyes opened wide in surprise when he raised his head and saw Hewie, through the glass window in his office. The man was just outside the window, in the engineering department, talking to a draughtsman. *I can't believe this*, he said to himself. Still, he hated to ask. Hewie looked busy. Lloyd bent his head and said another prayer. "Lord, have Hewie come into my office, if you would have me talk to him about a job for Don."

Two minutes later, Hewie knocked on the door of the office and entered.

"Hey, Lloyd, how are you doing, man?" Hewie shook his hand with a firm grip, smiling. "It's been a long time."

They talked for a few minutes, catching up on the latest news. Lloyd knew, of course, that he *had* to ask him about the job, but he couldn't muster up the courage to ask for a favour like that. After all, it had been just a short time since he had asked him if he had an opening for Mike, Susan's husband. "How's Mike?" he asked. "How are things working out with him at the plant?"

"Fantastic. We need more help—looking to hire more people." Then, after a brief goodbye, Hewie left.

As soon as Hewie walked out the door, Don's uncle came to his senses, as if he were waking up from a dream. *I've got to ask him about that job for Donny. God answered my prayer by sending Hewie to me; I've got to ask him.* He jumped up and ran out into the hall, chasing his friend down.

"One thing more, Hewie. I have a nephew in Montreal who is looking for a job…"

"Send him down to Windsor and I'll interview him."

"It's a long way to come for an interview," Lloyd said.

"Well, then, send him down and I'll hire him."

Monika could hear the smile in Uncle Lloyd's voice, when he called to say that Don had the job.

Don started his job as a plastic-mould design apprentice in September. He and Monika felt a new lightness, when they left the city that held so many memories for them and moved to the smaller town of Windsor.

They were shocked that he had gotten the job so easily, at a time when unemployment rates were high and any kind of work was hard to come by. They could sense, somehow, that this was God's hand in their lives. It was like a breath of clean air blowing through that tiny crack in the door he had been led to open for God.

They began to make friends in the area. Don played hockey with a church team, who asked that all players attend the church at least twice a month in order to play on their team. He agreed. Eventually, he began to look forward to the meetings, and very slowly he began to be interested in what the Bible had to say. For the first time in many years, Don had Christian friends in his life.

But the dark cloud that had loomed over him in Montreal followed him even to this new place. His lawyer had told him, "You will be charged any day now. It could be days, weeks or months, but don't forget it will happen. A good job might help, might influence a judge to see you making an effort to change."

Waking up each morning to the possibility of facing charges was torture for Don. It was the fear of this, and the inevitability of it, that made the cloud seem darker each day.

He was at work one day, working at a drawing board next to a big window on the second floor. Looking out onto the quiet streets below, he saw three police cruisers come into his line of vision and pull into the parking lot of the building. He felt his heart beating in his chest, and his face going cold and pale. *This is it—they've come for me. How can I explain this to my boss? What about Uncle Lloyd, who went out on a limb for me and has no idea that his nephew is a criminal?*

Don was petrified, frozen to his chair, until he watched them stop one speeding driver, then another and another. He felt his heart rate gradually slow to normal, as he realized the policemen had chosen the parking lot for a radar operation. He was safe—for a while.

But from that day on, the need to tell someone about his past began to occupy his thoughts more and more. He knew the secrecy was destroying him. He looked for an opportunity to tell the right person.

He had been in Windsor for six months when he received a new assignment at work. His job was to clean up an area—an isolated back room full of equipment and tools. His brother-in-law was assigned there, also.

Mike was a quiet guy with a sand-coloured beard. Their jobs at the same company had provided him and Don the opportunity of becoming real friends. Their new assignment, and the hours working alone together, gave Don the chance he had been looking for. It about killed him to bring it up, but one morning, soon after they had started the job in the equipment room, Don took a deep breath and plunged in. "Mike, what would you think of someone who...?"

He told Mike what had happened, always using the third person. Somehow, it was so much easier to say, "*He* did this," and "*He* did that." Mike listened quietly, and his answers encouraged Don. For a few days, Don kept up the facade, always hiding behind the thin veil of this nonexistent third person, who was guilty of all these things.

Slowly, over the days that they worked together in the room, he confessed to Mike that he was that criminal waiting for his trial and sentence.

Mike couldn't hide his surprise. But he remained a steady friend to Don, and gave him good advice. "You can't keep this to yourself any more, Don. Tell people—especially those you're closest to.

You need prayer and a good support system. And they need to be prepared before the bomb drops, when the charges are laid."

Don talked to Monika and, together, they decided to tell their friends and relatives, starting with Uncle Lloyd. Then, they had to tell his parents.

To see what is
right and not to
do it is the part
of the coward.
−Chinese
proverb

16
Another arrest

Don's parents, Murray and Georgia, had a cottage in the Laurentian Mountains, north of Montreal. It was a large, lumbering house, really—too big to call a cottage. They had bought it, unfinished but full of potential, several years before. For Murray, it was a haven from the busy city and the emotionally draining work of pastoring a church. He loved leaving the noise and the problems behind on Sunday nights after church and driving into the mountains. They usually spent the night there and most of the next day.

The air was different in the mountains. Cool and fresh and smelling of pine, even on hot summer days. The cottage sat high above one of the hundreds of lakes in the region. Eighty-eight wooden steps led down the steep incline to a little dock on the water. Those steps took hours to repair every spring, after each harsh northern winter, but Murray loved the work.

They fixed up the cottage in their slow, comfortable way, with two old refrigerators here and a cast-off sofa there (and another one on the porch overlooking the lake). There was no elegance, but it was perfect for them, a place to find a brief interlude between stressful weeks.

The family chose a weekend that summer, a year after Don's arrest, to visit the cottage together. Don knew he couldn't keep the truth from his parents any longer. He needed to tell them the whole story. He waited until everyone else, even Monika, was in bed, and the three of them were sitting in front of the fireplace.

He told them all that had happened, what was pending, and how he expected the trial would go. As he watched their faces crumble in disbelief and shock, he stumbled over his words. Unwilling to go forward, unable to turn back, slowly, painfully, he recounted the entire story. It was the hardest thing he had ever done.

Murray sat there, watching the dying embers of the fire. Don, and then Georgia, had hugged him and gone to bed long ago. Still he sat there, praying, thinking. He thought again about Don's arrest. It took him back—thirty years back—to his youth, and to his own arrest.

Two police cruisers, sirens blaring, screeched around the corner. They had barely stopped when six officers jumped out and one of them pointed to the redheaded twenty-two-year-old. "He's the one," the officer yelled. "Get him in the car." The young man showed no surprise, almost no emotion, as he quietly stepped into the car and was taken to jail.

This arrest was no surprise to Murray. The stage had been set two months before, when he had left his parents' farm near Toronto and crossed the border into Quebec, "la belle province." Murray was the fourth son in a family of seven boys and one girl. They were members of the community church, but it wasn't until he was a teenager that he was really with confronted the claims of Jesus Christ. The message of God's forgiveness had such an impact on his life that he knew he had to tell others about it.

Just across the Ontario border were millions of people who needed to hear what the Bible had to say. But enthusiasm wasn't enough, he knew, so he enrolled in Toronto Baptist Seminary. There, he took Bible courses, and began to study what would later prove to be invaluable—the French language.

One warm day in May, soon after completing seminary, Murray boarded the train from Toronto to northern Quebec to start his new job as pastor at Noranda Baptist Church. He was startled that night, as he read the headlines in the Toronto Daily Star. The reporter described in graphic detail the story of a group of Christians in Shawinigan, a city in the heart of Quebec, who met in a rented store to study the Bible. A mob of a thousand people broke into the building, tore up the hymn books, turned the piano upside down, ripped up the Bibles and overturned the pastor's car in front of the building.

The article worried him. "What kind of trouble will I face if I work among these people who have no opportunity of hearing the gospel?" he asked himself.

It wasn't long before his question was answered. Soon after his arrival, he and some church members held an outside meeting. They had just begun, when two police cars arrived. They were immediately put into the cruisers and taken to the police station, where they were detained for several hours. The police chief returned, with a stern warning: "Hold this kind of meeting again, and we'll slap you behind iron bars."

Murray immediately consulted Max Garmaise, an experienced Quebec lawyer. Garmaise advised that the authorities had no legal right to imprison them for preaching on a quiet street. If they chose to carry on the meetings, they would not violate any Canadian law. But, unofficially, he warned Murray about the powerful religious opposition in Quebec, and said that if they continued this type of activity, he was sure they would be arrested.

Murray was disturbed and confused. He had always been taught to respect the law—even when he didn't fully agree with or understand it. On the other hand, he knew that God is the supreme authority. Many of God's greatest workers—Daniel, Paul, Stephen, Peter—had defied the laws of their times when they chose to obey God. Was he called to make this same painful decision?

Whatever the cost, he decided, he must share the message he had with these people. It was a decision born out of two things: his love for God and *his love for the people of Quebec. Made one Saturday morning in July, it was a decision that was to shape his entire future.*

Immediately, he went to the mayor to tell him that they planned to hold a meeting that night, and that they were willing to cooperate with the authorities as much as possible. While Murray still talked, the frowning mayor picked up the phone and called the chief of police. Murray went out to start the meeting.

He and his friends were arrested that night.

Murray rose up from his old brown easy chair and slowly made his way around the room to turn out each light. He thought of the time he had spent in prison, and then he thought of the months ahead for Don. First the trial, then years in prison. How many? Five? Ten? Twelve? His back was a little stooped, as he dimmed the last light and climbed into bed.

Remorse is the
pain of sin.
–Theodore
Parker

17

78 Charges

"What did you say?" Don gripped the phone, and squeezed it hard against his ear. But he could hear B.J. Cameron's voice—only too clearly. "Eighty-one charges?!" All related to grand auto, conspiracy and government fraud.

Cameron had been served eighty-one charges in connection with their auto-theft ring. Others had received charges, too, and all were summoned to appear in court on June 7, 1984. But why had it taken so long—two years—for the charges to come down? Cameron didn't know. It was an unusually long amount of time. It had been a year since Don had told his parents about his crime. Since then, his life had changed dramatically.

On January 30, 1984, Monika had given birth to a baby girl. He started keeping a journal for the first time that day:

Erika Elizabeth was born this morning at 8:32, weighing 7 pounds and 7 ounces. I was in the delivery room and it was the most incredible experience I have ever had. Monika suffered a lot of pain, but held up well. She looked so happy when they handed Erika to her. Erika was as bright and alert as a two-year-old, from the moment she was born.

He had begun working with teenagers, many of whom had similar problems to those he had experienced. He found he could relate to them, could counsel them concerning their problems with parents, with friends, with addictions. But he was effective only because he was different now. Gradually, week by week, he had learned what it meant to be a Christian, a child of God. His encounter with God had changed him so radically that he had an intense desire to let others in on the good news, especially teenagers who were as confused as he had been.

Soon after Erika's arrival, he resigned from the Windsor company, to begin working full-time for Youth for Christ, a national organization whose goals perfectly matched his own. They knew of his past, of course, and knew that he could be summoned for trial any time.

His mother didn't believe he would ever be charged. She said his files must have been destroyed or at least lost. Don wanted to believe it. By the time twelve months had gone by, then twelve more months, he began to think she must be right. Some miracle would happen. God had seen he was a different person now, and of course he wouldn't be taken from his wife and child and punished for something the *old* Don Heron had done.

Then—bang!—he received the call out of the blue from B.J. Cameron. Cameron wasn't convinced, when Don said, "I don't think I'll be charged." He said Don's name had appeared on nearly all of the eighty-one charges. He set up an appointment for the two of them to meet with their attorney in a couple of days in Montreal.

The timing was good—Don's sister Janice was getting married that weekend in Montreal, so they had been planning the long trip for months. Don and Monika packed their bags and drove the twelve hours with four-month-old Erika, and Susan and Mike and their toddler, Evan.

Don tried to focus on the wedding festivities, but was preoccupied. He kept wondering about the charges and what would happen next. He met with Randy Hill, who owned an ice-cream shop now. Then, later that afternoon, he and Cameron met with the attorney Ronald Savage.

"These charges are of a very serious nature," Ronald said, clearing his throat. "When the time comes, you are better off to say very little, even if it means doing more time." He made a gun with his fingers and pointed it to his head, looking Don straight in the eye. "The less said, the safer you are."

Don went to the downtown library to look for articles written about the arrests, two years before. He found two dated Saturday, May 8. One was in *La Presse*. The other, from *The Gazette*, read, "Police have arrested 13 people, seized more than $500,000 worth of deluxe cars....The eleven men and two women are to face hundreds of charges in court...."

Who would have believed that today, two years later, he still would not have been charged? It seemed unthinkable, now, to face dozens of charges from his past life. Even with Cameron charged, and the obvious certainty of Savage that the ball was about to drop for him, too, Don was more convinced then ever that it wouldn't happen.

They returned to Windsor. On May 31, five days after Janice's wedding, Don wrote in his journal:

> *At 2:00* P.M. *two detectives walked into my office at Youth for Christ. They served me with seventy-eight charges. They asked me to explain how it all happened—off the record. The reality has now hit.*

Don knew he must stick to the truth, no matter what. Savage and B.J. thought that his new obsession with honesty just complicated things. At the last minute, just before the June 7 trial, God led Don to a new lawyer, Richard Wingender. Richard was a

Christian and he shared Don's commitment to integrity, even though this could sometimes be a difficult and dangerous course of action to take.

Don took a deep breath as he and Monika entered the courthouse on the day of his trial. Richard had looked casual at their only meeting, in jeans and a T-shirt. Now Don hardly recognized him, with his glasses and double-breasted suit, moving confidently in and out of the courtroom, talking to the crown prosecutor, then to Don and Monika, who were waiting in the hall.

While they were standing there, Ronald Savage came running up, and began talking, loudly and angrily, about Don's plea. "You can't plead guilty," he said. "It would be a huge mistake. If you do, they'll lock you up and within thirty days you'll be sentenced—three to five years, at least, and then they'll use that evidence against all the others, who will be sentenced accordingly."

Richard answered him quietly. "Calm down, Ronald. Don's not going to plead guilty—but not for the reason you're talking about."

Once again, Don could see God's hand clearly at work. Don had planned to plead guilty to every one of the seventy-eight charges of which he was truly guilty. But since so many people had been arraigned, there were hundreds of charges before the judge that day. Unwilling to take the time to listen to a plea for each charge, the judge had directed each defendant to enter one plea, guilty or not guilty, for their whole package. Since the charges had been "stacked," in anticipation of the normal negotiating that would take place, Don wasn't guilty of all seventy-eight charges. The only honest plea was "not guilty." This chain of events would take the heat off, from the other men's point of view, and Don wouldn't have to compromise his beliefs.

Later, after Don's plea was submitted to the judge, Cameron stopped Don and Monika on the courthouse steps. "You're lucky you didn't plead guilty," he said. "If you had, you would be a dead man." He pointed to a man leaving the building. "And he's the one who would have taken care of it. I told the other guys that you hired a religious lawyer and were planning to plead guilty to everything. The guys were jumping five feet off the ground." That night

Don and Monika thanked God for, once again, making a way for them, when the way seemed impossible.

When Don arrived before the judge, he was simply asked to return to court on July 17. Richard explained that on that date there would be a communication of proof and then a preliminary hearing. His trial would be by judge and jury.

They were taken to the identification building—the same place in which he had been locked up at the time of his arrest. There they put his fingerprint on seventy-eight pages—one for each of the charges. His picture was taken, then he was weighed.

The officer who took his information looked surprised when he said he worked for Youth for Christ. "You're lucky to have Christ for your lawyer," he said. Don wondered if he was being sarcastic.

"I didn't know Christ when I committed these crimes," he explained.

"So now you've been washed in the blood of Christ."

"It sounds like you know Jesus." Don said. It was more of a question than a statement, really. He wasn't sure which way to take the officer.

Then the man's face broke into a wide smile. "I've known him for four years. I understand how you feel. I wish I'd known him, too, before I made some mistakes of my own."

Monika watched through the window from the waiting room. She saw the conversation and the smiles. Smiling was the last thing she felt like doing. Watching the officer fingerprinting Don, she had a foreboding of how their lives would be changed, once he was branded a criminal. When he came out, she looked at him with tears in her eyes. Very quietly, she said, "This means you'll have a criminal record." They left the building silently, in a sober mood. Don came close to crying himself.

In prosperity,
our friends
know us;
in adversity,
we know our
friends.
–J. Churton
Collins

18
Waiting

It became clear to Don why God had allowed the beginning of the trial to be postponed for two years. The next months, driving back and forth between Windsor and Montreal for his court appearances, were extremely difficult. He was grateful that he had had the months leading up to the trial as a time of preparation.

After the arrest, for a long time, he had been terrified of the future. He thought he could never survive prison, that he would rather take his own life than end up there. He felt sick to his stomach whenever he saw a luxury car or passed the Jacques Cartier Bridge—anything that reminded him of his crimes, and the penalty he knew he would be required to pay.

Then he came upon the verse, *Seek first His kingdom and His righteousness, and all these things will be given to you as well.* Gradually, during his time before the trial, he had begun to trust God with his life and with his future. For the first time in his life, external things, such as money and circumstances, didn't mean as much as eternal things, such as peace with God. His life was realigned, so that by the time of the trial he was a much stronger person, or more accurately, he was more aware of his own weakness and more dependent on God.

He and Monika were amazed at the way Christian people reached out to them during the time of the trial. His journal began to fill with descriptions of ways they helped:

> *Mike said someone left an envelope at his place for us. It had $50 in it.*

> *Since yesterday, many have said they will be holding us up in prayer.*

> *Many have asked about the results of our court date.*

> *Went to Carlo and Connie's for a barbecue. Stayed till 1:00 A.M. Had a great time. They are very supportive of our situation and have said they will help in any way possible.*

> *Felt very depressed and alone this morning. Last night I fell asleep on my knees. God feels one hundred miles away lately…I am convinced that God has a purpose for me going through this.*

On July 17, Don's second court date, Richard, his attorney, met with Lemieux, the prosecutor in the case, and Desrochers, the chief detective. Lemieux showed Richard pictures of everyone in the organization and explained each person's role. He pulled out a diagram of the ring.

"Heron is number two in the organization, just under Cameron," he said. He tossed photos out onto the table, all of them implicating Don. "We have all the evidence we need to get him two to six years in prison."

After two hours with Lemieux, Richard met Monika and Don.

"Start packing your bags, Don. Monika, you'll simply have to do without a husband for a while. I think the best deal we can possibly hope for is six months to two years."

When Don appeared before the judge, the court date was put off again, this time until September 4.

On September 4, the trial was remanded until October 9. Don was warned by other members of the organization that he better not consider pleading guilty now. They were trying to buy off a judge.

On October 9, Richard was able to get a remand for another twenty days. This was an attempt to have the case heard by Judge Mirand, a seasoned judge with peppery hair and cut-off bifocal glasses. He was the same man who had judged the terrorists who had kidnapped Pierre Laporte and James Cross during the FLQ crisis years before, and he had been lenient. Richard felt that this would be in their favour.

After much work with the prosecution, Richard and Don had negotiated down to a remnant of the charges—those that Don was guilty of. They had also decided on a trial by judge alone. A pre-sentence report was ordered to be conducted by a probation officer in Windsor.

Finally, on October 29, 1984, Don stood before the judge and pled guilty to thirty-eight charges. Although this was a considerable improvement over the original package, the reality was a little frightening. Each of these thirty-eight charges carried a possible maximum penalty of between ten and fourteen years in prison. He was told that he would be sentenced on January 21, 1985.

When he returned for sentencing, he received bleak news. Judge Mirand had been appointed to the Quebec Superior Court and could no longer hear the case. The judgment would now be postponed for two more months, and would be heard by Judge Marchand, who had a reputation for being one of Quebec's toughest judges. He was particularly hard in cases involving organized crime. Don and Monika committed the whole situation to God, convinced that his will would ultimately be accomplished in their lives.

We are not
punished for
our sins, but
by them.
−Elbert
Hubbard

19

The sentence

The day Don and Monika drove to the courthouse for the last time was bright and sunny, with a cool breeze. March in Quebec is still weeks away from spring, so they were dressed in their winter coats as they found parking after battling the heavy Friday-morning traffic and made their way toward the building.

They walked the two blocks slowly, intensely aware that this could be their last time together for many months. How do you prepare to go to prison? They had lain awake at nights discussing what Monika would do, where she would go, how she would care for Erika. They had worked through every detail. Still, nothing could prepare them emotionally for this day. They walked up the long steps that ran the entire width of the building that had become so familiar to them.

As they walked through the glass doors, they could see that it was business as usual. Here some of the elite of society—judges, defenders, prosecutors—deal with criminals, many of them from the lower echelons of society. From nine to five, they wheel and deal, trying to solve some of the most complex problems imaginable. The greater world of crime is seldom organized, more often sloppy and usually confused by contradicting witnesses.

They had arrived early, so they waited in the crowded cafeteria line and went through the motions of eating—loading their trays with bacon, eggs, toast and coffee. They left the food untouched, but were glad to have a few minutes to talk before the others arrived. Don's parents planned to be there, and two of his sisters, Janice and Carolyn. The director of Montreal Youth for Christ, Russ Hopkins, would also come and of course, Richard, Don's lawyer.

They met the others as they ascended the stairs on their way to the courtroom. Don handed his long trench coat to Monika and gave her one last kiss as he moved, along with Richard, to the front of the room. Courtroom proceedings got underway, and the crown prosecutor spoke first. He built a convincing case against Don, arguing that these crimes were premeditated and highly organized. Don and his partner had spent hours planning them, and had gone to bed at night reviewing how to carry them out successfully. As he effectively established reasons for a harsh sentence, he carefully avoided eye contact with Don.

Richard stood and argued in Don's defense—he was reformed, a very different man, had a good job with a benevolent organization, had a wife and a child. He had no past criminal record. He was experienced in law enforcement.

Don stood next, and asked the judge for leniency: "Your Honour, I recognize that what I did was wrong and I deeply regret having participated in illegal activities. My life has changed since I gave my life to Christ three years ago. I would never be involved in anything like this again. I fully recognize my error, and I'm more sorry than I can say."

Next came a surprise. The prosecutor asked if he could speak again. Don held his breath, as the man reclaimed the judge's attention. "Your Honour, I feel I must say a word on this man's behalf. The evidence is undeniable." This time he did look Don straight in the eye, just as he finished his brief speech. "I am convinced that the defendant is a changed man."

There was a moment of surprised silence, before the judge gave his decision. He shuffled his papers and cleared his throat. "I don't know this man. One of his colleagues was given a six-month prison term on many fewer charges. Considering the testimonies in the courtroom today, I am giving the defendant the same sentence: six months in prison for each charge to be served concurrently, a $5,000 fine for each of the charges also payable concurrently (six months to be added in default), and two years' probation, with the condition that he will not associate with B.J. Cameron or Randy Hill during that period of time."

In spite of Monika's tears and his parents' distress, Don felt a sense of peace as he was taken out the back of the courtroom. He was convinced this sentence came ultimately, not from the judge but from God.

Misery
acquaints a man
with strange
bedfellows.
—William
Shakespeare

20

A Bordeaux welcome

Don squinted through the murkiness of the truck, but the meshing made it impossible to see out the back. It was like an army truck, with a row of three benches along each side. *There were eleven guys in there, not counting the Lord*, he wrote, later that night, in his letter to Monika.

He had been acutely aware of God's presence with him, ever since he had been escorted out of the court into a holding cell. He felt as if God wouldn't let him forget his presence, when the guard, who had been curiously kind to Don while he emptied his pockets onto a steel stool, told him he was certain his six-month term would be reduced to two. Then, he said he knew Don's dad, Murray. "Don't worry," he said to Don. "It will all work out." To Don, he seemed like an angel.

After another wait, they were each handcuffed to another man, marched down a long corridor and loaded into the truck in which they rode now. As they headed toward the prison, Don studied the man he was chained to. He had a Mohawk haircut and wore a red bandanna around his head. On both sides of his head, where his hair was shaved, he had scars every few inches. Then Don saw the inside of his arms. He counted fourteen slash scars from his wrists to his elbows.

Slash, as Don silently nicknamed him, noticed Don staring at his arm. He said, "Guess how much it's worth." He must have thought Don was looking at his watch.

"At least a couple hundred dollars," Don answered quickly, figuring it was safest to shoot a little high. Slash looked pleased.

"I traded it for a pair of boots that were finished."

Later, at Bordeaux, during the routine questioning, when a guard asked him if he had any scars or marks on his body, the guy with the Mohawk threw back his head and laughed. Then the guard asked if he had ever tried killing himself. "I do that quite often," he answered.

"Well, don't try it in here," the guard answered. "We don't like blood." He assigned the man to A Wing, a special wing for older men, short-term men and psychiatric cases. Don hoped he would see him again; he wanted to talk to him about God.

The truck stopped with a jerk and backed up to the door of Bordeaux. The men waited together in another holding bin until they were called out, one by one, into a different area. When Don's turn came, they asked him to take off his clothes and proceeded to strip search him. Then they handed him a pair of blue jeans, a red T-shirt, work boots, socks and underwear. They kept everything but his watch and wedding band, which they permitted him to wear with his new prison uniform. He was glad about the ring—he felt Monika's presence there with him, every time he looked at it.

Later, on the inside, he would discover how rare it was for them to let a prisoner keep his wedding band. He would see only one other person wearing one—a well-known Italian singer named Johnny, who had been connected with the Mafia.

Don's first real feel for prison life came when they brought him into the huge hallway, sixty feet high, lined with three levels of cells

Don was sent to Bordeaux Prison, Montreal, to serve his sentence

on both sides. He was handed a stale sandwich and a cup of milk. As he stood there eating, the guys began to yell like wild animals—or a pack of wolves. When Don realized the yells were directed at him, his stomach heaved and he nearly brought up the food. *Don't put me in there with those animals*, he prayed. *Ship me to another wing.* But the guard opened the giant gate and Don walked into the room, feeling like a peewee in the Hell's Angels' clubhouse.

His cell was eleven by seven feet, with a steel bed, a mattress, a table bolted to the wall and no chair. The toilet had a sink over it, with one cold-water tap. There was a small window to the outside, and a peephole in the door. The door had no handle on the inside, a deadbolt on the outside, and he thought he'd never get use to that door slamming shut behind him. So this was the meaning of the prison term, *slammer*.

The lights went out while he was writing to Monika. He lay there, wide-eyed, sleepless, and tried to imagine her in his arms. The first night lasted forever, and he awoke to nothing more to look forward to than on the night before. His only thought was that right now six months seemed like a hundred years.

Randy Hill was in Bordeaux for the weekend. He had received a two-month sentence and was serving his time from Friday to Sunday of each week. This way he could keep his business, and keep his children from knowing about his prison term. Don saw him the next morning at breakfast—which was porridge that was nearly impossible to eat—and Randy introduced him to John Deer, a "speed freak" with gray hair and a beard, and Donny, a native with long, dark hair. Both were from A Wing. They pointed out a man who had been burning off his tattoos with cigarettes, by butting them on his arm.

John and Donny began saving a place for Don every meal, telling whoever sat down to get out of Don's spot. John told Don about his brother, who was an officer in the Salvation Army. He said his brother had written to him the week before, signing, "your brother in Christ." John wrote back and signed, "your brother in jail." John threw back his head and laughed at his own joke.

Don looked around the cafeteria. Never had he seen so many tattoos, scars, black eyes, missing teeth, blank looks or wild stares. He had a moment of fear, then he remembered a verse and paraphrased it in his mind—*Even though I walk through the valley of the shadow of death, I won't be afraid of any evil, for you (God) are with me.* He told himself that he would try to see these men differently, see that in spite of the rough exterior, every inmate in there was crying on the inside. He knew it from personal experience—he was in the same boat with them.

He was certain that God had sovereignly placed him in Bordeaux because his life could make a difference to someone else's. In his letter to Monika that night, he wrote, *I am more convinced than ever, that this is where God wants me.*

No untroubled
day has ever
dawned for me.
—Seneca

21
Letters

For the first few days of Don's incarceration, Monika stayed in Montreal with family and came to visit him. He was glad she was close by, during those days. When she went back to Windsor with Erika, he felt as if she was a million miles away. He lived for their phone calls, but money was a serious concern, and they knew they had to space them and keep them short. Besides, there was an unofficial prison law that you had to keep your phone calls down to fifteen minutes. If not, you just might get beaten up by another prisoner.

One of his most difficult experiences during those first weeks was a visit from Monika and Erika. Contact visits could not be arranged quickly, so they visited with a sheet of glass separating them. Don fought back the tears as fourteen-month-old Erika tried to kiss him. Her little lips pressed up against the cold glass and her eyes stayed focused on him. She looked so young, so innocent. How could he have dragged her into this? How could he ever make this up to her?

He found solace in writing to Monika. It helped pass the time in this place, where every day seemed an eternity. His letter writing became therapeutic for him, a way to make sense of all the things he saw and heard. Sometimes the place seemed unreal, and he felt that he would lose his grip on reality. But recording it all grounded him and somehow gave him the sense that these experiences weren't being wasted. He wrote to her regularly, sometimes even twice a day, mostly while in deadlock, the time prisoners spent locked alone in their cells.

Tuesday, March 26, 5:15 P.M.
We're in deadlock right now till 6:00 P.M., which is suppertime. I saw my social worker today. He seems like a nice guy....He said I should be classified in B Wing and will probably move tomorrow. I was just starting to feel at home in this cell. Most guys stay in this wing for ten to fifteen days....B Wing is supposed to be for offenders under twenty-one years old or those who have no record. Rumour has it, however, that the guys in B Wing are pretty tough and use a lot of muscle to get what they want.

Everybody's got a story in here and everyone seems to have a fair amount of problems on the outside, too. It's easy to read guys—one day they'll be up and seem real happy, and later they'll be in their cell all down and out. It's sad to see people hurting so much. I think of this place being built in the early 1900s—around 1914—and realize that guys have been crying out from here all those years and they'll keep crying out for years to come. I found out today that they started hanging guys here when Bordeaux was built, and the last man hung on March 11, 1960.

There's a guy named Ray, an older man, maybe forty-two or so— not that old, I guess. Anyway, he's like a big Montreal gangster, at least he talks that way. Kind of a nice guy, but he's torn up over marital problems....I was in the phone room the same time as him. One minute he was cursing her out, then the next thing I knew, he said, "You know I love you, babe."

10:30 P.M.

Back under deadlock. I spoke to you tonight and was so happy to hear your voice. I had been thinking about you and praying for you all day, as I knew you were travelling back. Tomorrow morning, I get my envelopes and stamps, so I'll mail this letter out first thing.

I talked earlier about guys being up and down. I guess I'm no exception. I've been through a lot of things and have lived in strange situations, but never have I experienced anything that comes close to this....The guys in here are all flipping out when they find out what I do for a living. There are a lot of liars in here and sometimes I feel guys don't quite believe me when I tell them I work for Youth for Christ.

Well, I better get this letter ready for sending, as I want to send it first thing and lights will be going out in about ten minutes. I just pulled out the picture you left me and I can't believe what a beautiful family I have. Erika is adorable and I just want to hold her and have her little arms around me. Give her a big kiss for me.

You're a beautiful wife, darling, and I'm getting all choked up just writing these things. I'm so sorry things had to work out this way, and I realize things must be ten times harder on you. I wish I could bear the pain for both of us. You're a wonderful wife and I'm very proud of you....I love you, darling, and continue to pray for you.

The next day, a man got beaten in the shower. There was a committee meeting over it just before deadlock that night. Each wing had committees made up of prisoners—the "heavies"—who ran the wing and "kept peace." If one inmate had a problem with another, he was supposed to come before the committee. If they felt it was a good "beef," they allowed the two guys to fight it out, usually outside.

The committee decided that the man who was beat up in the shower could settle accounts the next day.

Don wrote,

I've been reading Till Armageddon, *by Billy Graham, and God is using the book to speak to me in a very real way. The book opens up with a quote by Merv Rosell: "God could have kept Daniel out of the lion's den....But God has never promised to keep us out of hard places....What he has promised is to go with us through every hard place, and bring us through victoriously."*

The Lord is my only strength in here. Everything about this place is of the flesh. The stories, the jokes, the language, the dope, the pornography, the hatred, the violence, and even the tattoos. Guys in here have tattoos of skulls, Satan heads, Nazi emblems, vulgarity and women.

One week after arriving at Bordeaux, Don wrote a three-part letter:

Thursday, 10:00 A.M.
Yesterday, I made a frame for our family picture. I used paper for the frame and soap as glue. It works quite well. I also made a calendar and glued it to the wall with soap.... I now have a bottle of shampoo, emery boards, two paper pads, my envelopes (I'm allowed ten per week), two pens (I traded a chocolate bar for my first pen), and I also bought a few Pepsis for a treat every few days.

I've started doing some weights and sit-ups, too. It helps pass the time and I figure it's a good time to start getting in shape. Must go, but will continue this letter later. I love my girls. XOXOX
4:10 P.M.
I'm in deadlock right now. Yesterday afternoon, I was transferred to B Wing and I'm now in my new cell. I've learned a whole new meaning to the word hellhole. I'm in a small, darkish cell, with no chair and no locker. No more luxury for me. Even now, as I write, I'm kneeling on the cement floor. Everything was filthy dirty when I came in here, but I've cleaned it up a bit already.

For some reason, I took the move quite hard. Maybe because when I first arrived here, some guy told me that the committee here is very tough and runs things the way they want. He said that he's been in a few prisons, but has never seen anything as bad as B Wing in Bordeaux. He figures it's because a lot of these guys from eighteen to twenty-one are trying to make names for themselves and want to prove how tough they are. Last night I witnessed a fight. The president of the committee came out of the fight with a handful of long hair that had skin and blood on the end of it. He jumped up on a table and started waving it around as he screamed that this should be an example to anyone else who goes against the committee... I just happened to read Matthew 6:34 last night. It says, "Therefore do not be anxious for tomorrow; for tomorrow will care for itself. Each day has enough trouble of its own."

The whole feeling in this wing is different, and as I was cleaning my room, I began to feel a lump developing in my throat.... As soon as we were in deadlock, my emotions just seemed to erupt. For some reason, I just started sobbing. I began crying out to God to get me out of here and asking why I had to pay for the sins of my past. I tore down a pornographic picture that was pasted to the wall and pleaded with God to get me out of here.

God began to comfort me as he has promised through his Holy Spirit. I finished my cleaning and pasted our family picture and my calendar on the wall. I used the calendar to cover a drawing on the wall of a skull with a Nazi helmet, blowing flames.... I was suddenly impressed to continue this letter. I realize that for now, writing you is my only real escape from this prison. Thank you for being there for me, darling. You're a very brave woman and I love you dearly for it. I wish I could give you the world; you deserve it.... I'm not so much convinced that I am here, at least for now, to minister to these people, but rather, I feel I am here that through them God might minister to me.

Already, I have learned some important lessons. For one, I now have a clearer vision of a world dying without Christ. And second, I have felt and seen only a morsel of what eternity without Christ would be like.

I don't know what God has in store for the rest of our lives, but I do know that this is part of his perfect will. This is simply a part of our apprenticeship and we must live it to its fullest. Everything we learn through this experience, we will carry for the rest of our lives.
10:45 P.M.
We're back in deadlock for the night and I'm sure I will sleep like a baby—tonight I received your birthday card and letter. It was like a breath of fresh air, even with the tears running down my face. It

was great talking to you tonight. I pray that God will help guide you through the paying of those bills.

I found out that after the incident in this wing last night, some heavy metal came down. This morning, the guards searched every cell (turned everything upside down), and strip searched everyone. ...After supper, the committee called a meeting. It was just like the movies. All the guys gathered on the main floor with the committee and about thirty anciens (elders—guys with a bit of time in) up on the second level halls on both sides of us.

They introduced us to the president, the vice-president, the treasurer, the secretary and the president of sports. The president explained as meanly and with the worst language he could, that they were pretty unhappy. He said that someone had squealed on them about last night and that they would no longer be collecting debts or giving protection. He said they would only enforce the laws of the wing....He hoped guys would start settling their own debts and that when guys start getting punched out they will not step in. He said that if a fight breaks out in the TV room, not to stick around to watch or you'll receive the same treatment.

Last I heard, there were eight fights in the TV room tonight. There will be a few black eyes at breakfast tomorrow.

I spoke to my buddy, Ray.... He claims to have been here when the last man hung. Said they used to hear them trying the gallows with sand bags. He said they spent one solid week in deadlock prior to the hanging and a few days after.

Well, the lights have gone out and I've written the last half page out my window with the light of a security spotlight mounted on the (outside) wall. It's quite difficult, so I'll close for now and mail this first thing tomorrow...After talking to you tonight for nearly twenty minutes (on the phone), I found out that the phone I was on is exclusively used by committee members. That's proof enough for me that my guardian angel is bigger than any of these guys in here.

Don talked the guards into getting a chair for him the next day. He sat on it and read more of his Billy Graham book. The first words he read were a quote by the nineteenth-century Christian author Phillips Brooks, "I do not pray for a lighter load, but for a stronger back." Dr. Graham wrote that trials make some people bitter and other people better. Don sat and thought about that for a while, and concluded that even though he had thought he was prepared for his trial and imprisonment, he had still let some bitterness creep in—bitterness against the judge who had put him here, and against a society that would demand such a price from a man who was no longer a criminal.

All along he had been asking God to lessen his load. Why hadn't he kept Don out of prison? Maybe God wanted to strengthen his back. Don was beginning to realize that he could become either bitter or better through this experience, and it was his attitude that would make the difference. He thought of the words of the apostle Peter, something like—*Go through the furnace, and when you go through the furnace to the glory of God, the Spirit of God comes upon you, and there is a joy in your heart and you glorify God.*

Art, a man to whom Don had leant a book, was transferred to Don's wing. When he saw Don, he talked enthusiastically about the book—he had read half of it already and couldn't wait to finish it. Art hated the new wing, hated the aggressive behavior of the inmates there. "I'll be a nervous wreck when I leave here," he told Don.

Don met a boy who looked much younger than his eighteen years. "My dad is in C Wing," he said. "They wouldn't put us on the same wing 'cause they said he would be a bad influence on me. That's a riot—I've lived with the man all my life."

It was Friday, and Don was certain a shipment of drugs had come in. He saw one guy unwrapping some cocaine early in the evening, and after supper, while they were watching a hockey game in the TV room, the men in the front row were smoking hash. Half the men on the wing were spaced out. It seemed to Don that there was more junk in prison than on the streets.

That night, a man got badly beaten with a broom handle in the shower room. A rumour went around that the whole wing would be put into a forty-five day deadlock. For Don, the worst thing about it was that it would mean he would miss his call to Monika the next day, his birthday.

He that flies
from his own
family has far
to travel.
−Latin proverb

22

Birthday at Bordeaux Beach Hotel

The best moment on Don's birthday came when he woke up and found that there was no disciplinary action taken against the prisoners as a result of the previous night's violence. He wrote to Monika in the morning:

> *Since I've been in here, I have noticed FTW written on the walls, chairs, doors…In fact, those letters are scratched six inches big into the paint on the inside of my door. The sheet metal under the paint is black, so I have it written in big black letters. Anyway, these letters are always in your face and they stand for "F—— the world." That seems to be the theme in here.*
>
> *I hope my letters are getting through to you. If not, I'll have to stop telling you about the internal functions of the joint.*
>
> *A fellow told me that he is eligible for an early-release program, but before they qualified him for the program, they made him sign*

a sheet saying that he would not go to the press or media to talk about this place. That's why I'm not sure about these letters. They may, however, just scan them quickly, unless they have reason to do otherwise.

Today, I heard a guy bad-mouth one of the guards for something. Within five minutes, three guards came in and escorted him into another room. The guards were rolling up their sleeves as they led him away. Fifteen minutes later, the guards came out laughing, but with no prisoner. I've heard rumours, but that's the closest I've come to seeing it. If that kind of stuff really goes on, then these guards are nothing more than gangsters themselves.

I talked to a guy today who was walking and acting like he was in slow motion, wasted. I heard that 2,000 Valiums came into this wing last night. That would explain why everyone is so relaxed today.

He ended the letter with a poem for Erika, and asked Monika to sing it to her for him:

> *You're Daddy's little girl—*
> *As good as gold,*
> *As bright as silver,*
> *Luckier than wood.*
> *That's why you're so good,*
> *'Cause you're Daddy's little girl.*

After he closed the letter, he added a postscript:

> *Word is starting to get around that I'm a Christian. One guy asked me if I was into church. Another guy asked if it's true that I read Billy Graham books.*

The man who asked Don if he went to church was named Pat. He said to Don, "You have an innocent face, man. I was like you once."

"What do you mean?" Don asked.

"My parents were Christians. We all went to a Baptist church. Now look at me—somehow I ended up in the slammer."

116

"I was a prodigal, too, but I found out it wasn't too late for me to change. It's not too late for you, either—it never is. That's the amazing thing about God—he doesn't give up on us."

Prodigal. That word kept returning to Don's mind, describing his life perfectly. Now he was certain it described so many others in here, as well.

The prodigal in the Bible was the son of a wealthy man, who loved his boy with all his heart. But the boy had a wild streak in him, and he wasn't interested in settling down to work on his father's estate, like his older brother. So he asked for his inheritance early. When his father gave it to him, he took it and left, hoping never to return to the confines of his old life.

The young man went crazy with his new-found wealth. He ate the best foods, drank the best wines and surrounded himself with friends who lived the good life with him. But eventually, his money ran out and when it did, so did his friends.

He found himself alone, feeding pigs for a living, so hungry that he could even eat the pigs' scraps. He was hungry, filthy, cold, miserable, and he smelled as bad as the pigs.

He woke up one morning, as if out of a bad dream, and said to himself, *My father's servants live much better lives than this. I'll go to my father, beg his forgiveness, beg him to let me be his servant.*

He dragged himself, one weary step after another, back to his father's home. But he thought there was no way his father, whose heart he had broken, would receive him back as a trusted servant.

The old man saw the boy coming from far away and recognized, past the rags and grime, the gait of his son. He jumped up and ran toward the boy, arms outstretched, tears streaming down his face. His father's open arms were the first thing the prodigal saw when he returned home.

Don knew why Jesus had told this story in the Bible. He knew first-hand how hard it was for someone who had turned his back on the Christian life, to come back. It seemed impossible to overcome the barriers of cynicism, embarrassment, unbelief and uneasiness with other Christians and bow before God again and ask his forgiveness. And it seemed impossible to imagine that he would forgive and accept someone back who had blown it so badly—done so much to hurt him. But then, as in the biblical story, the Father's love is beyond our wildest imaginings.

How could Don help these men to understand the depth of God's love for them? He looked up, and cringed when he saw FTW scratched in black on his wall. Then his mind gave new meaning to the initials. *Why did Christ go to the cross?* He asked himself. *For the World. FTW.* From then on, every time he saw the letters, he thought of the new phrase, *For the World.*

It tears me up to think that Christ died for...not only nice, clean, educated people, but everyone, he wrote on his birthday. *I now see the cross more clearly as Christ hangs there—with a common thief on either side of him. They could have been two of the boys from B Wing. As he's hanging there, he tells one of them that today they will be together in paradise. What a perfect example of Christ's love for us!*

Before lights out that night there was more excitement. Five men from B Wing broke out of a back entrance near the TV room where the men were playing ping-pong, pool and cards. The inmates were ordered to their cells immediately.

When he reached his cell, Don looked out of his tiny window. He saw nine or ten guards with helmets and clubs scouting the fence, and a rope or wire hanging over the wall, on the side facing him.

As he stared silently out of the window, the whole place erupted like a volcano. The men on the wing went wild, kicking their doors and screaming insults at the guards. The echo against the cement walls and metal doors magnified the noise a hundred times. A voice came over the P.A. system saying that if the inmates were quiet, they might be out of deadlock by morning, otherwise, they would be in their cells for at least forty-eight hours. The men got even wilder.

One man was so out-of-control that the guards tried to enter his cell to stop him. When they opened the door, he jumped one of them and two other guards came running. They dragged the guy out. Don could hear the man screaming as they passed his cell. "Hang me! Hang me!"

Don went to his table and started writing another letter to Monika.

Things seem to have quieted down a bit. It's 11:00 P.M. and there are fewer guards running around now. I wonder if the guys made it out. We'll probably hear tomorrow or read it in the Gazette *Monday.*

My guardian angel is working overtime this week. Today at lunch, Art and I sat at the president's table. We were right into our meal, when some guy said, "Hey, that table is private." We picked up our trays to change places and as I stood up, I came face to face with the president himself.

The elders have privileges here, too. At supper, Art and I were eating and some guy came, put his tray down and said, "There's someone eating here." Art misunderstood—thought it was a question and said, "No, go ahead and sit down." The guy said, "I said there's someone eating here." Art and I immediately got the idea and moved to another table. In here, if you stand up to one of these guys, you stand up to twenty of them the next day in the shower.

He went to sleep, the night of his twenty-seventh birthday, and dreamt he had a piano in his cell, with all the time in the world to practice. When he was finished playing the ivory keys, he stepped out of the barred door onto thick, red plush carpet. Bordeaux had turned into the Queen Elizabeth Hotel.

The man who,
in a fit of
melancholy,
kills himself
today,would
have wished
to live, had he
waited a week.
—Voltaire

23
Reborn

The next day, Don learned that two men had attempted suicide during the pandemonium of the night before. One inmate had squeezed his head between the bars of his window and kicked the chair away, trying to hang himself. The other had broken up his Bic razor, pulled out the blade and repeatedly slashed his wrists.

Don stood in the corridor and squinted through the window into the second man's cell. Deep red streamed down the side of the toilet, and spattered the dirty floor. He remembered the first day, when the guard had said, "We don't like blood here." He could hardly keep down his lunch.

Terrified of being beaten up, nine men went into protective custody—self-imposed deadlock. The guards said that if ten people request protective custody, the prison officials automatically have to call in the Quebec provincial police riot squad. Don pictured the squad marching in at the steel plant, and shuddered. The thought of facing them here, especially now that he was on the opposite side of the law, was not a happy one.

Each day that passed seemed like a month, so Don checked it off on his homemade calendar, just to assure himself that time was moving forward. Two things made the prison term bearable. The first was his phone calls to Monika, and their letters. He wrote, *I just spoke to you a few hours ago, honey, and it did two things to me. First, it makes me very happy, because I love you very much and I want to hear your voice and know that you and Erika are all right. Secondly, it makes me very sad because I want to be home with you, helping you, supporting you and loving you. I want to be holding Erika, playing with her, teaching her, reading to her and loving her.*

The second thing that kept him going was his prayer time with God, and his growing conviction that it was good for him to be in here. Good for him, and good for others, if he could make himself available to God to touch their lives.

Over the monotonous days, he continued to get to know Pat the Prodigal, as he called him in his mind. Pat asked him questions such as, "How do you know for sure God's really up there?" And, "Is it possible for *anyone* to really change, or just certain guys?" And, "If a guy (Don knew Pat was talking about himself) has a woman and a nine-month-old baby, how can he clean up his act for them?" He went to "church"—a meeting in the chapel with the prison chaplain on Sunday morning—with Don, asking his questions all the way. Don nicknamed him Preacher, and Pat seemed pleased.

Don lent more books to Art, who read them and lent them to others. One night, Art and Don were talking, when a new guy came up and asked if Don had a book to lend him. Art said, "He'll give you a book to convert you." Don laughed out loud, that contagious belly laugh that always had others laughing along.

"Yep," he said. "I'm praying for the conversion of the entire prison population."

It seemed to Don that this place was the perfect place for people to find God. After all, it was pretty hard to be convicted of a crime and continue denying that you are a sinner. Everyone needs God, but, let's face it, the average man often isn't ready to admit it. Many of these prisoners had hit rock bottom. They had been brought to their knees by the courts, and now, maybe, they were ready to fall on their knees before God.

Also, they were desperately seeking freedom. When a man neared his release from prison, he became a different person. Don could almost spot which men would be released the next day. They were the ones bouncing, not walking, with a large smile on their faces. For him, it was the perfect picture of someone being freed from the strong iron bars, the long heavy chains, the stifling stinking cell of sin. That's what it was like for him. His sins had enslaved him, and now, even while he sat locked in his cell, he was as free as a soaring eagle. When he saw these men, how desperate they were to be free, he prayed they would understand that freedom went beyond the stamp of approval from a parole board.

Don first met Fast Eddy when he visited Don's cell and saw Monika's picture. He rolled back his eyes and took a deep breath. "Who says you have to die to see an angel?" he said, a broad smile planted on his wide mouth. Don liked him immediately.

"I'm reading a book you might like," Eddy said, noticing the books on the table. "It's about a guy who was really into crime, then he got reborn."

"What about you? Are you reborn?" Don asked. Saved and born again were common terms. But *reborn*—he had never heard that term before, and he liked it, especially the way Fast Eddy said it.

"Nah. You are, though, aren't ya?" Don nodded. "I thought so. My mom and my sister are reborn. Sometimes I think I'm close. But I'm just too shy. Anyways, my family pushes me too much."

They talked about world news, and the political situation in Quebec, then, more importantly, prison food and politics. "I guess you signed the petition, too?" he asked Don.

"Of course. You think I'm crazy?" Don answered.

After the fighting over the weekend and the last committee meeting, B Wing's president was placed in "segregation" for observation. It meant that he was put in deadlock in another wing. He declared himself a political prisoner, suffering for the cause of prison rights and, somehow, managed to circulate a petition for his release. The man who brought the petition to Don said that he'd better sign it—the president wanted the name of anyone who didn't. Don thought that was ironic, coming from a man who was so concerned about prisoners' rights.

The next day, Fast Eddy spotted Don at breakfast. "Good morning, brother!" He said, shaking Don's hand.

Brother. It made Don wonder…"Did you find the Lord last night?" He asked Eddy.

The same broad grin spread over his face. "A bit man, a bit," he answered. Don grinned back. Well, a bit wasn't everything, but it was sure better than nothing. He hoped that Fast Eddy was opening up to God, like he had that night after the meeting in Montreal, when the door had opened a crack. Don told Fast Eddy what a man must do to be saved. He could tell Eddy was listening.

Pat the Preacher came up to Don, practically running in his eagerness to talk to him.

"I prayed to God last night, Heron. I asked God what I was doing here, and could he please help me get out? Then, today, I heard from the parole board that I might be released early. My girlfriend came to visit today, and I told her I wanted to start going to church. She said okay, she'd like that. I'm not quite ready to give my life to God all the way, but I'm thinking a lot about it."

That night before deadlock, Pat stopped in to see Don in his cell and borrowed two Christian books. He said it was the only kind of book he wanted to read.

For a while it looked as if the petition would work and the president, along with his elders, would be released from deadlock. Then the secretary of the committee left Bordeaux on a stretcher, after a suicide attempt. He was pronounced clinically dead, as they rushed him to the hospital, but they managed to revive him there, and he was returned to the prison and held in "the hole."

That night TV camera crews invaded the world of B-Wing. They moved around the wing curiously, questioning the guards about all the weekend trouble. Fights, breakouts, suicide attempts, near riots—the word had gotten out. The men watched the report eagerly on the six o'clock news, straining to see a glimpse of them-

124

selves on TV. Don was glad he hadn't been around for the cameras. The thought of having his prisoner's face distributed on the TVs across Canada didn't make him happy. All the old committee members remained locked up, so the inmates voted in a new committee.

Not long after, Don browsed around the library for a few minutes, then stepped up to the desk to take out a couple of books. The inmate who worked there looked up. "Don Heron!" He said. Don jumped back in his surprise. "I'm Lachance—David Lachance. Don't you recognize me?" Don didn't, really. He wore a beard, now, and looked much, much older. Don could hardly believe he was one of the two brothers who had worked in their ring.

"Aren't you the one who moved to Toronto and got religious?" He asked, and Don laughed.

"Nah—moved to Windsor and got religious."

Lachance told Don that B.J. Cameron was in Bordeaux, too, in E wing with a two-year term, a $5,000 fine, and three years probation. Don was eager to see B.J. again, to find out how he was doing. But the judge had made it clear that no future contact was to be made between them. It seemed ironic that they would then both be sent to Bordeaux. Maybe he could find a way to lend him a book from his collection, which was quickly becoming known as the "Heron library."

Of all the inmates borrowing books, the one whom Don felt closest to was Art. He was often in and out of Don's cell, just to discuss something he had read. He returned *Born Again* by Chuck Colson, and asked if he could borrow *Life Sentence* by the same author. He flipped through it on his way out of the cell, and said over his shoulder, "If I don't get born again after reading this one, I never will."

One pardons to
the degree that
one loves.
—La
Rochefoucauld

24

Good Friday

The twenty men were unusually sober as they filed silently into the room for the Good Friday chapel service. Don nodded at B.J. across the room. Chris Carr, the chaplain at Bordeaux, asked them to sit on the floor around two roughly cut pieces of wood nailed together. The wood formed a life-sized cross.

Like a huge magnet, the cross drew their hands irresistibly toward itself, and they touched it, one by one, feeling its rough surface against their palms. Chris began reading, softly, his voice deep and full of emotion. He read about Jesus, healing the sick, giving wine to the thirsty and sight to the blind, lifting the humble and scalding the proud with burning hot words. Then, about Jesus being hunted by those who hated him, betrayed by the kiss of a friend and captured. An unjust trial and a merciless sentence—the cruelest of all sentences. An angry crowd and a heartbroken few.

Two crosses. One that held a repentant man, promised life; one that held an unbending man, doomed. And the third cross, the Cross. Holding the hopes and fears of all the years before and after. Offering, demanding, questioning, inviting, suffering, loving. God's anger. Darkness. Lightning. Thunder. An earthquake. Satan's fear.

A soldier who spat, and cursed and gambled. Another who fell to his knees and believed. Open wounds and wine-red blood. Jesus trembling, the crowd jeering. Jesus thirsting, the crowd mocking. Jesus weeping, the crowd cheering. Wildest celebration in the presence of deepest agony. Then Jesus speaking: Father, forgive them. Silence.

Don looked around the room at the twenty men and saw the crowd. He saw thieves and liars. Sex offenders, addicts, criminals. He thought, *what a bunch of losers*, and then, reflecting off a shiny gold plaque on the wall, he saw himself. He knew, then, that there was no offender in the prison worse than him, and no offender in that crowd on that dark day any more guilty. He felt the cross beneath his fingers and when he looked, he imagined he saw a nail there, too, and a hammer. And he saw, clearly, *his* hands driving nail into flesh. His own sin pounding mallet to table, with the terrible finality of the judge's penalty: Death.

Chris read on, and bits and pieces filtered through to Don's mind: *He (Jesus) has appeared to put away sin by the sacrifice of himself…So Christ was offered once, to bear the sins of many.*

As Don left the room behind B.J. Cameron, Chris told them to go down to the next floor and look through the curtained window. He told them they would get a good view of the hanging gallows from there. They descended the stairs and found the window. At first, when they pulled back the curtain, Don couldn't make sense of what he saw. Then, suddenly, it became clear to him. He wrote about it in a letter to Monika that night:

> *Now high above the yard, B.J. slid open the window. The feeling was awesome, and I had to catch my breath. There, seven or eight feet away and four or five feet above us, was the steely mechanism that for forty-six years swallowed one life after another. The structure was cold and ugly, especially on such a rainy day. My mind flashed*

images of men walking through those big red doors and of what must have gone through their minds as they stepped out onto the balcony. The balcony is in two parts, one small protruding area with a gate behind it and a floor that drops open in two parts from the middle out. The trap floors were hanging open. The other part of the balcony is longer and is where the hangman and priest would stand during the execution. Suddenly, my mind raced and began putting pieces together. Here I was, standing at an execution site on the day we remember Christ going to the cross. The feeling was so overwhelming that words could never explain it.

All I can say is that here in this house of unrighteousness where Satan's power is so evident, God took me back to the cross and showed me how very real his love is for me. Now as Friday comes to a close, I can hardly wait till Sunday to celebrate the resurrection. If God's only purpose for bringing me here was to show me the cross, it will have been worth it.

When he finished writing and lay down in the gloomy darkness of that Good Friday, he felt as if his spiritual senses had been opened. The cross had always been there, but now he could see it so much more clearly, could feel its power so much more deeply. It was like suddenly hearing the grass grow beneath your feet, or seeing the sun shine on the other side of the globe.

25

Easter without Don

Monika put a purple barrette in Erika's soft brown hair and pinched her cheek. The barrette matched her Easter dress. "Do you want some cereal?" She asked.

Fourteen-month-old Erika shook her head emphatically, her lips tightening into a tiny pink prune. "No."

"Do you want to go to church?"

"No," she answered, just as emphatically.

"Do you want to go back to bed?"

"No." Now Erika looked sadly serious.

"Do you want a pretty Easter egg?"

"No."

Monika laughed. Erika was learning new words every day now, but *no* was still her favourite. She also said *nite-nite*, and *bye-bye*, and *dada*, whenever Monika showed her a picture of Don.

It seemed strange going to church on Easter Sunday without

Monika and Erika during Don's incarceration

Don. She tried to put Erika in the nursery, but she screamed and clung to Monika so tightly that Monika couldn't bear to force her. She carried her into the church service and held her in the back row. Heather and Lindsay were sitting there, and Cindy with her new baby.

Monika looked at Cindy's baby and secretly thought that Erika had been a prettier newborn. Then she smiled as she remembered a comic strip she had seen. A mother, holding her baby, says to her husband, "Isn't he the greatest baby in the whole world?"

"I'm sure every parent thinks that," he says.

She answers, "That's true. But ours really *is* the greatest baby in the world!"

Well, she and Don agreed that Erika was the best, so that was proof enough for her. But Erika had been more difficult lately, fussier and more complaining. Monika had been awakened by her crying at night and felt edgy about the loud wailing, because she knew it annoyed the people in the next townhouse. Whenever the crying started, they blasted their music back at her.

Her friends tried to be helpful—they were constantly inviting her over for a meal or a cup of coffee, but Monika was seldom in the mood to go. She wanted to hole herself up in the house, wrap herself up in a cocoon, until Don's release. For her, spring wouldn't really come until then. Easter was painful for her, with all its memories and its associations with new beginnings.

Don wasn't there to share the fun of a holiday, and he wasn't there to help carry the responsibilities of daily living, either. The load of caring for Erika, paying the bills and explaining why her husband was in prison, was weighing pretty heavily on Monika by the time Easter rolled around, and she didn't feel much like celebrating.

She accepted her sister-in-law's invitation for supper. She and Erika ate and quickly left, and she had the feeling, possibly mistaken, that after she left, they said, "What's wrong with *her*?"

She sat down and wrote to Don the minute she got home that night, and then again the next morning:

> *I want you to know that I truly love you…more every day. When I hear women say they get tired of having their husbands around, I can't relate to that whatsoever.*
>
> *I was just thinking of you today, especially. This time apart now has made me appreciate you even more. I always have thanked God for giving me such a good husband and father. You'll probably never really know how happy you make me, and how much I really do love you.*

I have too great
a soul to die like
a criminal.
-John Wilkes
Booth

26
Hard time

Time in Bordeaux was creeping along for Don, too. And the worst thing about it was his separation from his two girls. He missed Monika and Erika more than he could have imagined. By now he had a small collection of their pictures on the wall in his prison cell.

Don stared at the pictures for a while, then moved over to look at his homemade calendar on the wall. He marked off another day. He could hardly believe he had been in this place for only three weeks. It was like when you're a kid, waiting for the big day when you'd wake up to find the bottom of the Christmas tree piled high with good things. Every day seemed like an eternity to you, and every day your mom complained about how quickly the time was flying, and there was still so much to do before Christmas. He imagined people on the outside, looking at their kitchen calendars and saying, "Can you believe how quickly the past three weeks have flown by?"

He knew time was passing slowly for Monika and his parents, as well. It couldn't be easy for them, knowing he was in prison and explaining it to their friends. Monika told him how difficult it was to explain to people that he was in prison for crimes he had committed in the past, and that he was different now. She sensed that some people who didn't know them well suspected he had gone to Windsor to run from the law, and the police had finally traced him there.

He was concerned about Granny, too, and how all this had impacted on her. When he mentioned her to his parents on the phone, they said he should call her.

Each time Don saw B.J. Cameron, he seemed increasingly lonely and unhappy. He told Don that he never received visits and that he had no one to call. "And I'm in the wrong wing. I don't belong here. If I could get transferred from C Wing to E Wing, I'd fit in much better."

Don told him he'd pray for him—that maybe he'd be transferred to E Wing, and he gave him three books, including *The Cross and the Switchblade*, about the ex-gang leader, Nicky Cruz. Nicky had been an "impossible case" from the social workers' point of view, but not from God's. After his encounter with Jesus, Nicky's leadership abilities took a very different direction. Don wondered if B.J. was another Nicky Cruz.

The next morning at breakfast, Don saw B.J. He told Don he had been reading the Nicky Cruz book—couldn't put it down—and he had been transferred to E Wing. It meant that Don would probably see him every morning at breakfast, because men from the two wings ate together.

27
Granny

Don's Granny Dalzell was not surprised, like all the other relatives seemed to be, when Don went to prison. She felt God had been preparing her for that, had told her, in the quiet way he always spoke to her some place deep down inside her, that Don's imprisonment was bound to happen. And she had been through this before.

Her daughter—Don's mother, Georgia—had always been a comfort to her. Early on, she had wanted to follow Jesus. She had grown up and married a preacher and had been a wonderful mother to her five children.

But Georgia's youngest brother, Bill, was a different story. He had been wild, even as a boy. He had run off to join the army at fifteen, where he had started drinking heavily. He had had several encounters with the law as a teenager, and when he was still young he had stabbed a man in a bar. The man had died eventually from his wounds, so Bill had been charged with "bodily harm with intent to kill" and sent to a prison for the criminally insane. When a man went into this place, it was said, there was no return. Often he was kept there for life.

One day Bill had been sitting in his cell looking at the sky through his window. He had remembered something his mother said exactly, just as if she were there with him: "If ever you're in trouble and nobody can help you, remember God can help you."

So after a very long time of never speaking to God, he had said, "God, You know my mother. You may not know me very well, 'cause I haven't been around much, but you know her well. If you get me out of here, I'll never touch another drop of liquor." Bill had been released later that year, and he had kept his word.

During his wild years, and while he was in prison, Granny had felt her heart would break, but she had never given up on him. Now it was Georgia's turn to stand back and watch her son go to prison. It hurt to think about it, but it was a fact and it had to be faced. Sitting there worrying about it wouldn't change a thing. So she prayed, and she read a book.

It was Chuck Colson's *Born Again*, the same one Don would later pass around in prison. As she read, she replaced Chuck's name with Donny's. That way she could picture him in prison and begin getting used to the idea.

She was watering her spider plant one night, commenting aloud that the long string of baby spiders trailing to the floor was getting entirely out-of-hand. The shrill ring of the telephone interrupted her remark. She picked up the receiver. " I have a collect call from Don Heron. Do you accept the charges?"

"Granny?"

When she heard Don's voice, she was taken back, as she often was these days, to another time, another place. This time her memory took her back twenty years, to when Grandpa was still alive.

"Grandpa, the kids are coming. They'll stay overnight while Georgia and Murray drive out to Val d'Or for the meeting. They can help you with the school floors and the garbage, but don't singe any of their eyebrows at the incinerator!"

"What's that you're saying about cows in the refrigerator?" Grandpa Dalzell yelled back at Granny. And she laughed and kissed his white head, as she filled the refrigerator with bottles of Coke for the kids.

He was a little deaf and sometimes it was inconvenient. But, all in all, it was probably a good thing, because she was a terrible snorer, and even on her worst nights when the bedroom shook like an earthquake was coming on, he slept like a baby.

He had been a mine worker, until he broke both legs in an accident in the mine shaft. Never able to return to mining, he became a school janitor instead, and they moved into an apartment in the basement of the school building. When the grandchildren came to visit, he let them help him with the cleaning. Donny loved the huge floor polisher, so Grandpa always let him try it. But it was a powerful machine—a monster to little Donny— and it went wherever it wanted to go, usually into the nearest wall. Never once was Donny able to control it, even after Grandpa's patient lessons.

Carolyn, Donny's youngest sister, always asked to ride on the cart when Grandpa carried the garbage to the incinerator. One time he even let her help toss the garbage in, but the heat singed her eyebrows and that worried Granny.

When the children arrived, she gave them each a quarter and sent them across the street to buy some candy. They loved coming here. They stayed often—whenever their Dad had to preach out of town. Sometimes it was for a day and sometimes it was for a week. But the school with the big gym was like a second home to them, and Granny was their second mother.

That night they piled into Granny's bed and she sang to them. They were songs that only she sang—songs she had learned many, many years ago when she was little like them—and she sang them until she drifted off to sleep. Then she started snoring and they watched her, giggling. They woke her up and she started singing again. The next thing they knew, the sun was peeking through the windows and Granny was still singing, but now she was in the kitchen.

The kettle boiled and she gave them tea, with lots of milk, and toast. Every morning, when they were at her house, she gave them tea and toast. She was the only person in their lives who thought it was just fine for little children to drink tea.

The kids played in the big gym until their parents came to get them. Grandpa yelled goodbye at them and waved, and Granny gave them each a big hug and told them she loved them. Then she went back inside and knelt at her chair to pray for each of them by name, one by one.

"Granny?" Don's voice pulled her out of the past. "How are you? It must be a shock for you that I'm here in prison?"

"No, Donny," she said, and she thought of the Chuck Colson book. "I read a whole book about you in there. God told me you would go there."

He sounded relieved, and very, very sorry. "Granny, I feel like I've really let you down."

"No, Don. You're supposed to be there. I know that. God has a very important mission. Don't miss it. You pray there, and I'll pray here."

And after they hung up, that's exactly what she did.

Men are not
against you;
they are merely
for themselves.
–Jan Christian
Smuts

28

If these walls could talk

"This is a very old prison, and I'm starting to find out that it has a real reputation," Don wrote to Monika in mid-April.

> *They say that it used to be a federal penitentiary, maximum security. That would explain the hanging gallows. They apparently would chain the guys down each night in these very cells. Foster has just finished reading a book called* L'Enfer de Bordeaux *(Bordeaux Hell)." He's going to send the book to me—if they'll let it in, that is. But he says he can't believe the things that went on here. My dad knows someone who works at a hospital near here and they say that every day they have guys rushed over from Bordeaux who've been beaten up. I guess if these walls could talk, we'd hear some stories.*

> *April 12*
> *Life continues as normal at Bordeaux Beach. We had a little excite-*

ment here yesterday. You see, the worst thing a guy can do here is steal from another inmate. They call them cell rats. If anyone finds out about a cell rat, they're supposed to do him in. I mean, give him the best beating they can—or kill him. So, yesterday, two guys had their cells ripped off. One guy lost a carton of cigarettes and the other guy lost some tobacco and chocolate. Anyway, the committee decided they were going to find the thief, so they conducted a complete cell search in the whole wing. They didn't find the goods and have concluded that a guy must have somehow gotten in here from another wing. I find that hard to believe. I think maybe it's a cover-up, as they may have discovered it to be an elder or a committee member. I mean, let's face it, there are not too many honest people in here....

I think I've now witnessed the ultimate in contradiction. There's a guy in here who on one arm has a tattoo that says F.T.W. On the other arm, he has a picture of Christ with a crown of thorns on his head and drops of blood, with the words around it, "In Memory of My Friend."

Have I told you about Gary? Don asked Monika in another letter. *He's been a heroin addict for ten years. He's only twenty-seven years old. He says that his habit used to cost him $200 per day and his girlfriend had a $100 a day habit. He said that even then, that amount of heroin was just enough to keep them straight and not high. He's never had a serious job, so he always had to raise that money by hook or by crook....He spent Christmas at another prison, and because he didn't have heroin, he went cold turkey. He says he spent days on end in his bed with the shakes and throwing up. He said he could never have done it on the outside, because the whole time he was sick, he knew that all he needed was a fix and he'd be normal. Had he been on the outside he would have done anything for that fix.*

I have spoken to him a lot about the Lord and he says that he is looking for the truth, as he's tired of all the bull that the world has to offer. He feels that he won't be able to resist heroin when he gets out, but says he will only do it on occasion and never make it a habit again. I find that hard to believe, and I'm sure he doesn't believe it himself. Heroin is available in here. When the guys are out on a weekend pass they swallow syringes that have been reduced in size and the needles are capped. It's expensive, though, so I think he might have only shot up once or twice in here. He amazes me with his knowledge of medicine. He knows where all the stuff comes from, what it's made of, and most important, how to get it. It's so sad to see a human being wasting away like that. He needs a miracle.

He felt a miracle *was* happening in Art. Don was walking down the corridor one day and heard—or thought he heard—the strains of a hymn that he had known since he was a child. He stopped in his tracks and stood listening, perplexed. He followed the tuneless, but recognizable hum back up the hall and to the left and found Art, humming the hymn, reading his fifth book from Don. Don grinned and started humming with him.

They talked and talked, and Art lapped up the conversation about God like a thirsty man in the hot desert sun.

Don had ordered two of the books in French. As soon as they arrived, he gave them to Stephan, who had discovered reading while he was in prison. A few days before, he had read two and a half books in one day.

The day after receiving them, Stephan returned one of the two books to Don. "What did you think of it?" Don asked.

"I loved it. I get goosebumps just thinking about it." He told Don about his girlfriend—they had been living together for six years and had a two-year-old son. She had left him for another man, a friend of his, and had broken the news to him just two days before.

Don listened to story after story that sounded much the same. It seemed that every time he called Monika, someone nearby was raging into the phone, often cursing, stamping, even kicking the phone, angry with a girlfriend or a wife who was leaving or had already left while the man was serving his prison term.

He felt so sorry for these guys. He believed it was one of the main reasons for attempted escapes from Bordeaux. He saw some of that same frustrated energy when they played hockey.

I've learned a whole new meaning to the term contact hockey."
We've started playing ball hockey in the outdoor rink. They leave
the boards up and you play with no ice. Anyway, the boys are wild.
No referees and anything goes. One guy was on acid, so I guess he
couldn't feel anything, cause his hands were all cut up and bleeding.
I was in the game three minutes and I got a stick across the face. It
swelled up around the eye, but the swelling's gone down. It's a little
blue and a bit sore. Anyway, I kept playing, but spent more time
getting out of the way of sticks than anything else. The team I was
on lost and the boys took that pretty hard, too.

Listen to a
man's words
and look at the
pupil of his eye.
How can a man
conceal his
character?
—Mencius

29

Eye transplant

Don had had several conversations with Gary, the heroin addict he had written about to Monika. He had shared his own story with him, telling him about the change God could make in a man's life. Even so, Don had a little trouble believing that much could be done to change Gary. Of all the inmates that Don had come across in Bordeaux, Gary had to be one of his least favourites. He had become increasingly annoying to Don, as the days went by. Everyone said he was a bum, and Don couldn't think of a better name to describe him. He was always bumming something off someone—from a cigarette to a bite of a candy bar to a *Playboy* magazine. Don found himself cringing whenever Gary came within twenty feet.

He had done the same sort of thing on the outside, too, only he hadn't asked permission to take other people's things. That's how he had ended up behind bars. Unemployed and desperate to support their $2,100-a-week habit, he and his girlfriend had robbed stores, broken into homes and picked pockets. Each morning when they woke up, they came up with a new scheme or planned to try an old trick in a new place. Sometimes, the girl would lure the pharmacist out onto the floor of the pharmacy, and Gary would silently slip behind the counter and lift the drugs he wanted.

One night, while Don was writing to Monika, Gary slunk into his cell and stood, slightly stooped, in front of him. "I got somethin' to ask ya, Heron—a favour." He spoke with a hint of a whine in each word, as if the whole world and everyone in it owed him something. Don felt a wave of intense dislike sweep over him.

Swallowing the urge to tell him to get out, he put down his pen in his right hand, while he covered the letter he was writing with his left hand. "Sure, Gary, what can I do for you?"

"Gotta go back to court tomorrow. For somethin' I did—you know—a while ago. I can't even remember what it's all about now. Anyway, the cops don't forget. Gotta go before the judge tomorrow and I'm scared, man. I'm scared." His voice trailed off in a nervous whimper. Don was amazed that he could muster three distinct moods—cool nonchalance, angry defiance and patient suffering—in one short speech, and still manage to end with his habitual whine. He reminded Don of a weasel he had once seen, writhing with his foot in a trap.

Can't help you, there, I'm afraid, he wanted to say and continue on with the letter. But he remembered Jesus' words about those who needed help: *For I was hungry and you gave me something to eat, I was thirsty and you gave me something to drink, I was a stranger and you invited me in, I needed clothes and you clothed me, I was sick and you looked after me, I was in prison and you visited me....Whatever you did for one of the least of these brothers of mine, you did for me.*[1]

He would try to see Gary differently. This poor man stood before him, wallowing in the misery of the life he had created for himself. At twenty-seven, he looked old and used up, as if the drug he so desperately sought had sucked the life out of him and tossed him away.

---

[1] This text is actually speaking about ministry to other believers, but Don was still a young Christian in his understanding, at this point.

"What can I do to help, Gary?" He said it in a softer tone.

"Feel kind of funny asking, man. Just wondered if…Just thought maybe you…wouldn't mind praying for me tomorrow morning. When I'm in court, I mean." Then he slunk away, as quietly as he had come.

Don went to sleep that night, haunted by those words he had remembered from the Book of Matthew, *Whatever you did for one of the least of these…you did for me.* He promised himself he would pray for Gary tomorrow.

The guards came for Gary at 5 A.M., long before the other prisoners were up, to take him to the courthouse.

A good night's sleep has a way of erasing the previous night's events, and Don passed through his entire morning without one thought of Gary entering his mind. He ate lunch and then went back to his cell and for some reason fell asleep. As he drifted off, a picture of Gary, standing in a courtroom, floated into his mind. He jerked awake, sat up in bed, and looked at his watch. It was 12:30 P.M. *Gary has probably already been sentenced*, he thought, but he started praying anyway. Asking forgiveness from God because he had forgotten Gary, he prayed, *Help him to be aware that you are there with him and that he is not alone.*

Actually Gary had waited all morning for his turn in front of the judge. He was finally called into the courtroom at 12:30 P.M. The facts of the case were presented. As he was taken back to the bullpen, the small room where the accused awaited sentencing, Gary's lawyer explained that he would probably be given two months, added to the time he was now serving, and that he would be sentenced late that afternoon.

Before the guard could lock him in the bullpen, Gary was called back before the judge. After he shuffled into the room, staring at the worn toes of his running shoes, he raised his eyes to look toward the judge. He never saw the judge's face. As he looked up, his eyes were drawn irresistibly toward a crucifix above the judge's head. He stood, staring at the cross, incapable of looking away, the whole time the judge talked. He wondered if Don had prayed for him. Then he thought about all that Don had said about Jesus, and at that instant, he believed with all his heart that only Jesus could save him from his sins, from himself.

Gary heard the judge's voice, as if from far away, sentencing him to fifteen days in prison, to be served concurrently with his present sentence. This meant, in essence, he was given no time at all.

That night Don saw Gary, tall and no longer stooped, walking toward him in the game room. Don was struck by the obvious change in him, but as he came closer, it was his eyes that stunned Don. They were dramatically different. Clear and bright, they almost shone as he walked across the room. It looked to Don as if Gary had gone to the hospital for an eye transplant, rather than to court.

"How did it go, Gary?" he asked, staring the whole time at Gary's eyes.

"It went good, because I have God on my side."

After Gary told Don all about what had happened, Don called Art over. "Do you remember when I told you I prayed for Gary?" Art remembered and told Gary it was just after lunch, about 12:30. Gary's bright new eyes lit up immediately.

After Gary and Art walked away, Don sat thinking. He had had such an aversion to Gary before, could hardly stand the sight of him. Then, the previous night, he had seen him differently, had felt compassion for him. His vision had cleared and he had seen another person, the way Jesus did. Maybe Gary wasn't the only one who had gone away and come back seeing out of new eyes.

Many times, the
reading of a
book has made
the future
of a man.
—Ralph Waldo
Emerson

30
Yap! Yap! Yap!

Don nearly keeled over when he peeked into Steve Wilson's cell and saw him sprawled out on his bed, reading. He was lying on his back, one tattoo-covered arm behind his head, the other holding the book Don had lent him. He was completely absorbed in the final pages, sounding out each word in a loud whisper.

Tall, muscular, unrepentant and completely unreformed, "wild Stevie" was not a man Don would want to meet in a dark alley. But he had been hanging around Don's cell lately—said he liked to talk to Don because he was the only one who listened and talked sense.

Two nights before he had come to Don's cell, asking to borrow a *Playboy* magazine. "Don't have one," Don said, "but try reading this." He handed him *Run, Baby, Run,* the book about the gang leader from New York City.

Steve turned away. "Nah, I don't think so."

But Don called after him. "Try one page. Maybe you'll be surprised."

Steve didn't want Don to know he had never read a book before. He took it and read the first page, and then the second. *Too much work*, he thought, and decided to give it back to Don. Then he read one more page and got hooked. Now, two days later, he was nearly finished.

Don stood in the doorway until Steve looked up and shook his head. "Can't put it down, man," he complained. "Never thought I'd get into this kind of stuff." Art came into the cell just as Don was telling Steve about his encounter with God at the evangelistic crusade.

"Be careful, Don," Art warned. "If you get too many converts, they won't let you out of Bordeaux. You already have your own congregation."

Don didn't miss a beat. "You can lead the hymn singing."

But Art continued talking, "Watch out, Stevie! Don was a notorious criminal, but he got reborn and now he's a saint."

April 20
Yesterday noon, the guys were complaining so much about the food—how it's no good, it's garbage, my dog eats better, yap, yap, yap. I got so upset, I got up from the table, told the guys we were all here because we're losers, that not one of us was here because we are a winner and that this food was excellent, because by rights we all deserve bread and water. Then I walked away from the table. At supper, I sat with the same guys and they were all carrying on about how delicious the meal was. What a gang!

Because life was so intense in prison, every day seemed equivalent to a month on the outside. He found himself caught up in these men's lives—in their hopes for the future and in their problems and disappointments. He wrote about one of these men, whose name he never knew, to Monika:

While I was working on the van this afternoon, I saw a guy I had seen when I lived in D Wing. I hadn't seen him since then, but [then] he was a very happy-go-lucky guy. Very tall, with dark hair and good-looking. He was always laughing and walked with his shoulders back and a bit of a bounce. When I saw him today, his shoulders were down, he had no bounce to his walk and no smile on his lips. In fact, his face was so badly beaten that I barely recognized him. He told me that he ended up in C Wing, but couldn't talk long enough to explain what happened.

I met this guy here named Terry Lawson. He's an ex-Montreal Alouettes player....Anyway, his uncle is Stew Lawson, my old boss. I couldn't believe it. Terry's here on fraud charges that got him eighteen months. He's probably in his early thirties, has a wife and three kids. Owns his own promotion company and lives in Beaconsfield. He worked as a cop for the American army for a few years, too, and also did investigative work in Montreal

Stephan left yesterday. Before he left, I gave him a French Bible my dad had brought in. I wrote a little note in the front and took it down to his cell. The night before, he had told me how his mother had died when he was eleven, and that his father had given him up for adoption. Between eleven years old and sixteen, he lived in thirty-five different foster homes. Now he has lost his girlfriend and two-year-old son. He had been blaming God for his misfortunes. When I took him the Bible, he couldn't hold back the tears when he thanked me. It was a very touching moment. I believe that a seed has been planted in good soil, and in time it will surely grow. Praise God.

Some guy just started freaking out in his cell. I can hear him smashing at his door and screaming. The guards are coming, so I'll go to my cell door and see what's happening.

It's twelve midnight now and I just finished watching all the action. It was my buddy Franky, three doors down. I just met him a few days ago. He's only twenty years old, well built, good-looking, but a little spacey. I think he may have done heavy drugs in his day. He's in here on armed robbery and kidnapping, also threatening with a deadly weapon.

Anyway, they brought down five guards and a doctor and wheeled him out on a stretcher. It took a while and I heard them say he couldn't move any more. I just now heard an ambulance, so they must be rushing him out to the hospital.

Maybe he overdosed on acid or peanuts (Valiums). Some of the stuff that comes in here is real garbage. When they wheeled him by my cell, he had no clothes on, and he looked stiff as a board—just looking straight up. Now some guy is howling like a wolf. Some nights are worse than others in here. I think it may have to do with how much dope is in here. When the guys are high, it seems to have a devastating effect on them when they go into deadlock.

Well, my black eyes are pretty well gone. I fit in here pretty well for a few days, as they got pretty bad. Everyone thought I had gotten done in or something.

Chris Carr, the chaplain, told Don about a man who had committed suicide, hanging himself in "the hole"—solitary confinement. Don wondered if that, too, was connected with drugs. A guy in C Wing got stabbed, but survived the wound. Don heard that everyone in C Wing carried a knife or had one hidden in his cell.

The next day, Don saw Franky, the man who had been carried out on the stretcher:

In my last letter, I told you about Franky.... Well, I saw him today, and he looked fine. Turns out he faked that he was paralyzed, so that they would take him to the hospital. He told me that he felt sick, but didn't trust the doctor here, so figured he'd make sure they sent him to the hospital. What a guy! Everyone's a con artist in here.

My buddy, Steve Wilson, had a misfortune today. He owed a few hundred dollars for dope, so they did him in downstairs this after-noon. We haven't seen him, but rumour has it that he ended up with a severely broken nose and some bad cuts. He may not end up back in this wing, or if he does, he'll go to protective custody—P.C., as they call it here.

Tonight, the guards searched the cells of the guys Steve owed the money to, so everyone thinks he must have talked. That's a no-no in here.

Don had difficulty sleeping that night, thinking about the suicide and the stabbing and Steve Wilson. He vowed to talk to him the next day.

He knew that inmates weren't supposed to talk to someone in protective custody, so he waited till the others were at lunch and then slipped up to Steve's door. They talked through the tiny window, and Steve seemed glad to have a visitor. "You're gonna leave soon, aren't you, Heron?" he asked.

Don nodded. He hoped so, anyway.

"I need your address. Can you give me your address?" Don said he'd give it to him, and they talked for a few more minutes. As he turned to go, Steve pleaded with him again. "You'll find a way, somehow, to give me your address. Won't you?" Later, Don wrote it on a small piece of paper, rolled it up, and stuck it through a hole in the door.

Friday, April 26, 7:00 P.M.
I saw for myself today the awesome depression that follows being refused parole. There's this guy I work with in the bolt shop named Michel…. He's French-Canadian, happy-go-lucky, helps everybody and has a real neat laugh. Anyway, this afternoon he came back to work after going before the parole board. It was obvious he had been refused, as he walked over to his bolt table, grabbed a hand full of bolts and started throwing them at the wall. It only lasted a few minutes, as a guard went and quieted him down. He had been swearing furiously at the same time and once he was stopped, a cloud of deep depression seemed to settle over him. He didn't say another word for the rest of the day. He's not in my wing, but after work I was walking behind him, heading toward the hub of the prison. From the view I had of him several yards back, he looked like a different person. His shoulders were slumped, his chin almost rested on his chest and his feet dragged. In his misery, he looked ninety years old. His emotional state suddenly became very real to me and it was as though I could feel his pain. I felt a lump in my throat and I had to do everything to keep from crying. I actually wanted to go over and hug him like a father with a little kid and

tell him that life was still worth living. I can't believe it—I'm all choked up just writing about it. I believe that God may have given me a little taste of how he feels when he sees us hurting. I'll never forget it as long as I live—what an overpowering sensation.

It was about that time that Don learned for certain he had been granted parole and would be released on May 10, in two weeks. And he would be able to tell Monika in person, because she planned to bring Erika from Windsor for a visit on the last weekend in April.

It had been a while since Don had looked in a mirror, and he felt strangely shy about Monika seeing him in his wrinkled clothes and his uncut hair. But he could hardly wait.

The weekend visit came and went. He was subjected to a strip search after he left Monika—it was prison policy after each contact visit. He was told to take his clothes off and go into a small booth. There, the guard donned a rubber glove and checked every crack and crevice of his body. For Don, it was excruciatingly humiliating, but he knew the process was necessary because of the drug problem.

Drugs were so prevalent in Bordeaux, one would think they were piped in with the water. Desperation inspired addicts with ingenious schemes. Once he had seen two inmates cutting up human feces on a paper plate with a plastic knife, searching for drugs. He learned that when they got out for weekend visits, they would fill condoms with dope and swallow them, waiting eagerly for them to move through the body and magically reappear a few days later.

So the strip search was necessary, and as uncomfortable as it was, he knew it was worth it, if it was the only way he could see "his girls." He wrote about the visit later, in a letter to Monika:

Seeing you and Erika on Saturday was unbelievable. It was excellent—Erika has grown so much and changed a lot. She's such a little lady now, so mature and smart and dressed so cute. She was like a little fashion model. She reminds me a lot of her mother. I'm so proud of my two girls, it's unreal. You both make me very happy and I love you very much.

Patience is
bitter, but its
fruit is sweet.
−French
Proverb

31

Cell party

Don's reputation had grown during the two months he had spent at Bordeaux. He was with his friends, when a man he didn't even know came up and asked if anyone had cigarette-rolling papers. No one had any, and he said to Don, "I won't even ask you. I know you don't have anything like that." Don was surprised.

Someone said, "Heron, when are you going to start taking confessions in your cell?" Don just laughed in his contagious way, and they all joined in.

Steve Wilson remained in protective custody. Whenever he could, Don continued to slip up to his cell and give him a rolled-up note or whisper a message through the door. As he was climbing the stairs to see Steve one day, Don smiled, remembering an incident before Steve's beating and protective lock-up. While the guys watched TV, Steve ran a shoelace through Terry Lawson's belt loop and tied him to the bench. Terry was so embarrassed when he tried to stand up, he vowed to pay Steve back.

Payback time came in Don's cell. Terry tied Steve's feet together and tied him to the steel bed, then threw cold water in his face.

The next morning, again in Don's cell, Steve threatened Terry that he would get revenge. Terry tied his feet together again, carried him out to a garbage can and set him inside, bottom first. Steve was stuck, unable to get out, waiting there for several minutes.

By the time the two had finished that night, Don's cell looked like a tornado passed through it. But they surprised him by cleaning up the mess they had made and making his bed.

Don's cell had become a popular hangout spot. One night, while they were hanging around telling jokes, Terry Lawson suddenly got serious. "I don't know what it is about this place. It's always cozy or something. Maybe it's the pictures, or all the cards hanging there." Don was proud of his "card clothesline," as he called it. But he didn't think it was the reason the room felt cozy.

"I think it's the presence of the Holy Spirit," he said. "He's here with us, you know."

Once early in the week, then a second and third time, Don saw a tall man in his mid-twenties watching him. The man quickly looked away when their eyes met. Don asked Art his name and learned he was Paul Adams, one of the few English-speaking men in Bordeaux.

"Notice he's missing a finger?" Art added. Don hadn't noticed. "He tried to use that in his defense at his trial for armed robbery. The missing finger is his trigger finger, so he asked the judge, 'How could I have pulled the trigger without a finger?' Of course, he was wearing gloves, so his victim had no way of knowing there wasn't a finger under there. Anyway, the judge wasn't convinced, and he ended up in here."

One rainy Wednesday afternoon in the game room, Adams approached Don and introduced himself. Don had the feeling he wanted to say something, but couldn't get the words out.

Then again on Friday, the same thing happened. As Don watched Adams retreating, he couldn't shake the feeling that the man had something important to say. That night, Don looked up, just before lock-up, to see Adams standing in the doorway. "Have a seat," Don said. But Adams didn't sit down. He paced around the tiny room, biting his already stubby fingernails. Stopping suddenly, he said almost defiantly, "So you're religious, eh?"

Don sat looking at him while the question registered in his brain. It was a normal enough question. He had been accused before of being religious. But as he watched Adams, poised there, cheeks flushed, fists clinched, legs slightly apart and planted stiffly on the cold cement floor, the man's intensity, like an electrical current, conducted itself through his question right to Don's heart.

Am I religious? Everyone was thinking it, saying it. The verdict was in. Everyone thought so. He didn't think of himself as religious. He was just like everyone else in here, but had been turned inside out in his encounter with the God of the universe. He was every guy in Bordeaux. He was Steve, and Art, and he was Paul Adams— with one mammoth life-shattering difference. He was God's child.

Adams didn't wait any longer for an answer. He told Don about his Grandmother Adams, who was a born-again Christian. "I got saved when I was eight, you know. But it must have slipped my mind, because somewhere along the way I got off the path and went in the other direction."

His questions for Don seemed endless. He wanted to know all about Don's past life, his crime, his sentence, his faith, and above all, what he could do to get on track.

The answer came from somewhere down the hall: "Just get reborn!" It was Gary, who stormed into the cell and slapped Adams on the back. "That's what happened to me. All you have to do is ask Jesus to come live in you heart. But it's serious business."

Adams turned to Gary and asked him some of the same questions he had just asked Don. Then he turned back to Don. "How do you feel about being locked up? I can't stand this!" He looked around the cell. "Is it different, when you know God is with you?"

Now another voice answered from the doorway. Art's bass voice carried a hint of a smile. "I can answer that. I'm Don's private bodyguard and I've been watching him for the past two months. He doesn't mind being in here, at all, because God has sent him here on a mission."

Maybe not minding *at all* was a bit of an exaggeration, but Don was deeply moved by Art's words. They sounded faintly familiar, but he wasn't sure why.

That night, the guys stayed until they were forced to go back to their own cells. It was one of Don's last cell parties.

Just as the lights flickered and disappeared and Don lay in his bed surrounded by darkness, Art's words about his mission came back to him. He remembered, now, why they had seemed familiar. They were like those his Granny had said during their phone call the other night: "You're supposed to be there. He has a very important mission."

Sometimes, especially at night, he felt overwhelmed with loneliness. And sometimes, he felt fed up and frustrated with the men around him. He often felt weak and incapable of making any lasting impression on these guys. So what about this mission thing? He asked the question and nearly drifted off to sleep.

Then, in the darkness, a light bulb went on in his mind. He said into the night: *I may be weak and inadequate, but I'm not the point. It all goes back to God.*

These men are hungry for God, so God is at work in their lives. Doesn't it say in the Bible that no one seeks after God? So if they're seeking, it's God at work in their lives. And he put me here, in this place, to be involved in his work. To be a small part of the work he is doing.

The conversations, the cell parties, the books, they all played a part in the mission. But the most important thing about this assignment was that it wasn't undercover—he was no longer pretending to be something he was not. He was clear about who he was, for the first time in his life. And that, more than the books or discussions, was what seemed to have an impact on the guys.

That was his mission, maybe, but was it the only reason? He took a good look at himself. He had no mirror here, but what he needed to inspect wouldn't be reflected in a mirror, anyway. He was a different man than he was when he had entered Bordeaux, just two months before. God had not only used *him* to change the guys around him, but he had used *them* to change *him*.

As excited as he was to get out of this place and be with Monika

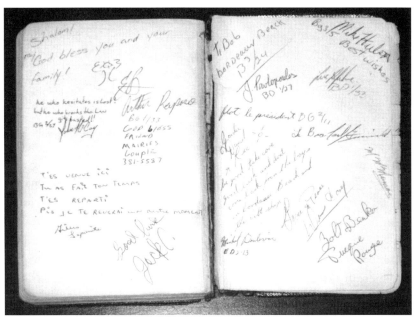

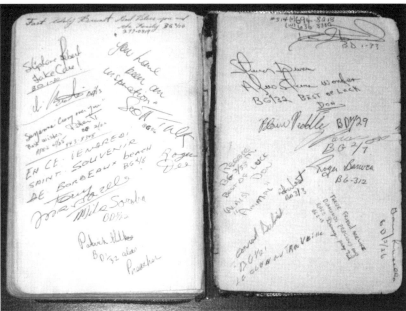

Don's Bordeaux Bible, with signatures and notes
from his fellow inmates and friends

and Erika, he missed the guys already. His last thought, in those fuzzy moments just before sleep, was that he'd get some of the guys to sign the front pages of his Bible. But his mind was too clouded to determine if this was a good idea or a ridiculous one, so he decided to wait until morning to think it over.

It took Don several days to get the thirty-five autographs in his Bible. He carried it around with him and sought out the men—at the pool table and the picnic table, in the weight room, in their cells, knowing they might not like their buddies standing around watching while they signed a Bible. Fast Eddy signed first, putting his prison ID number after his name. So each inmate who signed after also included his ID number. The men wrote little notes or well-known quotes. Don sat on his chair in his cell and smiled as he read each one. Then he moved his Bible, still opened, to the upper right corner of the table and composed his last letter to Monika.

I believe in
Christianity as I
believe that the
sun has risen,
not only
because I see it,
but because by
it I see every-
thing else.
—C.S. Lewis

32
Spring

When May 10, 1985, rolled around, he was ready with his brown paper bag—holding the entire contents of his cell. He sat in his best suit and waited to be called, tapping his dress shoe against the concrete floor in a quick, impatient rhythm.

Leaving Bordeaux was exactly like entering—only in reverse. After he was called, he waited in the same office and then was given back his pocket contents in an envelope by the same guard who had taken them away two months before. Then he stepped into the visitation area.

Monika and Erika looked too beautiful to be real. He hugged them both, all in one enormous bear hug. Then he kissed Monika, and took Erika, who was sixteen months old now, into his arms. She hung there, limp like a rag doll, staring at him with round blue eyes. He thought he saw a glimmer of recognition, enough to keep her from crying and lurching back into her mama's arms. But there

Monika's Welcome Home cake, celebrating Don's release

were no kisses from her, no laughing response to his smile.

Don's parents were there, too. They took Don and Monika to the car-rental place, then drove off with Erika, whom they watched for the weekend.

"Where to, now?" Don asked Monika, who was in charge, since she, with Janice's help, had planned this weekend getaway. He saw her gaze take in the myriad of wrinkles in his clothes, and he cringed. "Paper bag special," he said. His suit and tie had spent the past months in a tight little ball in a paper bag, and there was no iron at Bordeaux Prison. "You look wonderful!" Monika laughed, and by the look she gave him, he knew she meant it.

Later that night they ate supper at their same favourite chicken-and-ribs place, for old time's sake. There was no B.J. Cameron there this time, and they didn't miss him. It was just the two of them—with a lifetime ahead.

Their second honeymoon lasted two days. On Sunday, they met Don's parents and Erika at the train station in downtown Montreal. "Wave to Grandma and Grandpa," they coaxed Erika, as they boarded the Windsor-bound train. Murray smiled and Georgia blew them a kiss, while the train began to move away.

The twelve hours between Montreal and Windsor spanned a season as well as a province. It was a typical mid-May weekend in Quebec, no longer winter, but not yet spring. But as the train travelled west and a little south, Don watched spring come.

He saw the dark buds spread into glowing green blades just hours before they became full-fledged open leaves. The gray grass turned green, too. And the sky became bluer and the air warmer. Somewhere along those tracks, Don left the cold, dark walls of prison behind him, along with all the years of darkness and uncertainty. He had paid his debt to society, and now, finally, he could put it all behind him and start again. He felt himself, along with the train, move into spring. From deep within, his heart welled up and sang silent praises to his heavenly Father, who had given this prodigal another chance. He thanked God for a new life, a new beginning.

He looked over at Monika, asleep with sleeping Erika in her arms, her head leaning against the window facing south. Then he remembered what day it was. "Happy Mother's Day," he whispered. She didn't hear, didn't even stir. But she had a soft smile on her face, maybe because she had seen spring come, too, just before she had fallen asleep.

I have come
that you might
have life more
abundantly.
–Jesus

Epilogue
–by Don Heron

In some ways, that train ride back to Windsor seems like an eternity ago, and yet it also feels like yesterday. Fifteen months after our return to Windsor, we were blessed with our second daughter. Along with her sister Erika, Kristina is also the apple of our eye. Our girls have always been a delight and a source of inspiration to us. We have been fortunate that over the years Monika has, for the most part, been able to be a stay-at-home mom. Our children are a trophy to her great effort and to God's grace.

Since leaving Bordeaux, life has not been all sunny skies and blue waters. In fact, the clouds of life have blown in often, and in some cases they have been dark clouds and they have lingered. One such cloud came when I discovered how tough it was to obtain work with a criminal record. In the late 1980s, I helped pioneer an organization called Give Them A Break Ministries to help ex-offenders find work after their release from prison.

Don, Monika, Erika and their new addition, Kristina, in September 1986

We had moved to Kingston, Ontario, where we felt the ministry would be much needed. There are nine federal penitentiaries in Kingston, and so we moved our young family to a city where we knew no one. This proved to be a particularly hard time for us, as we soon ran out of money and desperation set in. At thirty years old, I took a job stocking shelves for minimum wage.

Two months later I answered an advertisement from the local newspaper for a sales position at Leon's Furniture. The potential income said "forty thousand plus per year" and I went to the interview enthusiastically. After being interviewed by one of the owners named Peter, I was told that I was ninety-nine percent hired. Peter asked me to come back the next day to meet his brother Mark.

The following day I was back in the store full of hope and expectation. I had told Peter in my interview the day before that I was involved with helping ex-offenders. When he met me on that second day, and as we walked through his store, he explained how they could never hire anyone with a record, because of the large electronics inventory. He then stopped and looked at me straight in the eye and asked, "You don't have a record do you?" My choices were clear, I could tell the truth and lose the job, especially since I was only ninety-nine percent hired at that moment, or I could lie and take my chances at losing the job in the future.

I looked back at Peter and said, "Yes, I do have a criminal record." For the next hour we sat in his office and discussed the difficult dilemma he was in. Then, as though ordained by God, he said "I'm going to hire you anyway, because I have a good feeling about this."

That day marked the beginning of a relationship with the three owners of that store, Peter, Paul and Mark McKercher, that has lasted and prospered for fourteen years. During that period of time I would also come to know Mr. Tom Leon and a fifth businessman named Dan Bengtsson. Possibly without even realizing their impact, these five highly successful men began to breathe confidence back into my life. They simply accepted me for who I was and believed that my future was more important than my past. I was acutely aware that God was working through them.

I have experienced God in many personal ways over the years. He has always proven himself, by sticking closer than a friend and by revealing himself in some way through the situations at hand.

In 1992, Monika was told by a neurologist that she had an enlarged blood vessel in her brain and that surgery would be necessary to repair it. It would be a very risky operation and an MRI was scheduled, in order to examine the problem more closely.

The crisis drew us together as a family, and we presented our need of prayer to our church. The congregation had a special time of prayer at the front of the sanctuary one Sunday morning for Monika. Shortly thereafter, the MRI was performed and we met with the neurologist to discuss the prognosis. When the doctor came into the room, he said that there had been an inexplicable change. He had two tests with very different results. The MRI showed no evidence of an enlarged blood vessel, and yet it had been initially very apparent. As we questioned him on this, he simply

Don's guest appearance on the TV show
100 Huntley Street **on November 10, 1994**

said, "There is no medical explanation, we will just have to call it 'the case of the vanishing abnormality.'" We thanked God for what we considered to be a divine healing. There have been no recurrences and no other problems in this regard.

I met opposition regarding my criminal record once again, when I tried to obtain a license to sell life insurance. Finally in 1991, after many near failures and thoughts of giving up, I was granted a tribunal, where I was tried on my previous criminal activities. The Ontario government concluded after fifteen months, both from their investigation and the tribunal that, in their words, I "was now a person of good character, who did intend to hold [myself] up in good faith as a life-insurance agent."

Over the next eight years I proceeded to sell life insurance, investments and related products. During that period of time, God showed us great favour and re-established us financially beyond what we would have imagined.

Three years ago I began to sense that God was preparing me for a new challenge. Armed with my belief that life is a journey and that success is a moving target, I accepted an invitation to go back to work for the McKercher brothers. I am now managing their newest Leon's franchise in Brockville, Ontario, and am also involved in a supervisory role at their Cornwall store.

In the past four years, I have become involved with Paul Henderson's ministry, the Discovery Group. I have been his point man in both Kingston and Brockville. This is a work that challenges businessmen to participate in one of the many weekly early morning Discovery Groups, where they can assess their beliefs, character and actions, consider the application of biblical principles and examine the claims of Jesus Christ. Paul has become a friend and an encourager, as well.

Today, I consider myself a very blessed man. I have a wonderful marriage, two great daughters who have decided to follow Christ themselves and a career that I love and find challenging.

As I write these final words, I must tell you that I am presently in the middle of another of life's storms. A year ago, I was diagnosed with follicular carcinoma, a rare form of thyroid cancer. My surgeries and treatment are nearly completed and the prognosis is good, as far as we know. This, however, is one of those dark clouds that could linger for many years. I do not know the future, but in recent months I have reflected a great deal on my life and my relationship with God. I am reminded of David, who defeated Goliath. Before he picked up the stones and proceeded to head down into the valley to meet the enemy, he paused and reflected on how in his past, God had delivered him from both a bear and a lion. I'm sure that these memories strengthened David's resolve with the challenge at hand.

As I reflect on my life, I realize that God has delivered me from

Don and Monika, with their daughters Erika and Kristina
on a family holiday, March 2002

life-threatening situations in the past, and so I have confidence to go forward. I can tell you with certainty that my present health issues have not caused my faith to waiver. As long as I can draw breath, I will profess and tell of the marvels of God and I will continue to enjoy that more abundant life that Jesus promised.

I am unable to conclude, however, without challenging you, the reader, to make your life right with God. It is a decision that will not only secure your eternal destiny but also one that will give you peace, joy and a purpose for this life. Ask God to forgive you of your sins and believe that his son Jesus Christ died for your sins and has been raised from the dead. Surrender your life to him. Jesus said that if you hold on to your life you will lose it, but if you give your life you will save it. Scripture goes on to say, "What will it profit a man, if he gains the whole world but forfeits his own soul?" Won't you follow Christ today?

January 2003

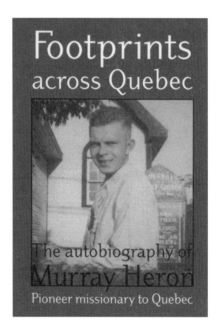

Footprints across Quebec

The autobiography of Murray Heron
—pioneer missionary to Quebec
By Murray Heron
Edited by Ginette Cotnoir

Footprints across Quebec is an engaging account of the progress of the gospel in Quebec over the past fifty years. It recounts turbulent days of overwhelming opposition to evangelism and preaching, as the province faced enormous spiritual and social upheaval. Murray Heron was powerfully used to open up television, radio and camp ministries to bring the message of Jesus Christ. This book communicates his steadfast commitment to his calling and offers a shining testimony to God's power throughout a long and fruitful ministry.

ISBN 1-894400-01-1, 126 pages, 6 x 9, perfectbound, softcover

Order online at www.joshuapress.com

Deo Optimo et Maximo Gloria
To God, best and greatest, be glory

Cover and book design by Janice Van Eck
Set in Interstate and Janson Text
Printed in Canada

www.joshuapress.com